Commentaries on James, I & II Peter, I, II, III John and Jude

Just the Basics Series

Discovering the Truth in an Untruthful World.

By
Danny Glenn Thomas

Bible versions are from KJV, NKJV, ESV, NLT, LIVING BIBLE and MESSAGE.
This book was printed in the United States of America.

To order additional copies of this book contact:

dannygthomas47@gmail.com

FWB
For Worthwhile Books Publications
Columbus, Ohio

Table of Contents

Commentary on James

By
Danny Glenn Thomas

Forward

Study to present yourself approved: Paul writes to his protégé Timothy in **2 Timothy 2:15** *"Be diligent to present yourself approved to God, a worker who does not need to be ashamed, rightly dividing the word of truth."* **NKJV**.

It is the duty of every believer to study the Word of God, The Bible, Scripture. The more one studies it the more confident he becomes in his life and the more vivid God becomes in his life. As the believer becomes more competent in God's Word the more useful he becomes in the work in which God has called him in spreading the Good News to others.

As the grandfather or Poppie, as my nine grandchildren call me, I have become more concerned about them. I want to be used of God in helping them to become more competent in their understanding of life and more consistent in their journey through life for the cause of Christ. To do this I fully know that they must know God's Word. In order to rightly know and apply God's Word, they must develop a consistent habit of studying the Bible.

I want them to start their growth as *"new born babes,"* **1 Peter 2:2**; with a great desire for the milk of the Word and then grow to enjoy the *"meat of the word"*, **Hebrews 5:12**. So, I have a great passion to leave my grandchildren a basic understanding of God's Word; to grow from this basic knowledge as a student to become a competent teacher of God's Word. **2 Peter 1:13** *"Yes, I think it is right, as long as I am in this tent, to stir you up by reminding you, knowing that shortly I must put off my tent, just as our Lord Jesus Christ showed me. Moreover, I will be careful to ensure that you always have a reminder of these things after my decease."* **NKJV**

That brings me to my desire for writing and my passion in writing these series of books: <u>Just the Basics</u>. I am leaving these with them and for you, the reader, as well. I desire not to make this commentary and exposition of God's Word to be an intensive one, but rather, one that would create a thirst to want to know more. I want to create a desire to seek further understanding and to make it your quest for greater knowledge of God's Word. I want this book to cause the reader to begin a personal search and study of God's Word; to make it your life quest to have a clear and competent understanding of Scripture. If this becomes true, then you will have become a help, a guide, a teacher of God's Word to others. I do not want to lean upon the opinions of others but rather, lean upon God's Word to interpret God's Word and depend upon the Holy Spirit to give understanding. If this becomes true, then my passion will have been fulfilled.

That is my quest, this is my desire. The Holy Spirit will give you greater understanding as you begin your study with <u>Just the Basics</u>.

Introduction

James is one of the brothers of Jesus as is Jude. Paul mentions James in his letter to the Galatians believers in **Galatians 1:18 & 19** *"Then after three years I went up to Jerusalem to see Peter and remained with him fifteen days. But I saw none of the other apostles except James, the Lord's brother."* **NKJV**

It is to be noted that James, though they shared the same mother, Mary, does not claim this honor to be applied to his life. Growing up with Jesus as a half-brother must have brought with it a great deal of rivalry within the family. We know that Jesus' brothers opposed Jesus during his ministry but after His resurrection things changed and the understanding of James and Jude changed in a huge way. **John 7:5** *"For even His brothers did not believe in Him."* **NKJV** The names of the brothers of Jesus are given in **Matthew 13:54 - 56** *"When He had come to His own country, He taught them in the synagogue, so that they were astonished and said, 'Where did this Man get this wisdom and these mighty works? Is this not the carpenter's son? Is not His mother called Mary? And His brothers James, Joses, Simon, and Judas* (Jude)? *And His sisters, are they not all with us? Where then did this Man get all these things?'"* **NKJV; 1 Corinthians 15:7** *"After that He was seen by James, then by all the apostles."* **NKJV** For James not to give mention of this is a display of great humility and understanding of position among other "believers".

The epistle of James is thought to be one of the earliest of the New Testament writings haven been written around A. D. 48 to A. D. 52. James gives the reader encouragement, instruction and caution for living of the Christian life with success and happiness. James is a very practical book within the New Testament give specific instruction in dealing with real life. The epistle is known as one of the "Wisdom Literature" of New Testament Scripture.

Chapter 1

"James, a bondservant of God and of the Lord Jesus Christ. To the twelve tribes which are scattered abroad." **Vs. 1**

Unlike Diotrephes, mentioned in **3 John 9** James did not seek to put himself first and above others of the church. James was content to be what God had called him to be and to be doing what God had called him to do. He did not compare himself with others or his ministry with that of others. When a believer places his eyes upon what others have accomplished wishing that they had that ministry or wondering why God did not place them in that ministry; then pride, lust and covetousness begins to build in their lives. James calls himself a bondservant of God and Jesus Christ.

A bondservant or bondslave was a slave that had been given his freedom but rather than leave his master he chooses to stay with his "good master" and remain as his slave or servant. We read the description of a "Bondservant or Bondslave in **Deuteronomy 15:16 – 18**. James calls himself a slave or servant by choice. He gives his total allegiance and life to his Lord and Master Jesus Christ. James does not look at anything other than what God has given him. We too ought to live our lives for Christ in such a manor.

The letter is written to *"the twelve tribes which are scattered abroad."* Soon after the church was empowered by the Holy Spirit it began to be scattered abroad to do what Jesus had called them to do; to make disciple of all nations. *"Therefore, those who were scattered went everywhere preaching the word."* **Acts 8:4 NKJV**

"The twelve tribes" are the Jewish believers of the church that were scattered or dispersed and also know as the "Diaspora". This specific group of believers were experiencing some difficulties of which James was aware and he therefore, he writes and sends this epistle or letter to them.

It may have seemed odd to these believers that they were being oppressed and the oppressors seemed to be winning over them. Why was this happening? Where was God, may have been the question or at least thought that was preeminent in their minds.

We must remember, God is always in control even when we think he is not with us at all. God will never leave us or forsake us. Because evil seems to be happening, God will with that evil intent bring about His will and good will come from any evil a believer might encounter.

Remember Joseph talking with his brothers in Egypt? In **Genesis 50:20** *"But as for you, you meant evil against me; but God meant it for good, in order to bring it about as it is this day, to save many people alive."* **NKJV**

We cannot see the future but God does and He also see today. We must take comfort it this and also in the fact that nothing can happen to us but that has not been filtered through the loving and all sufficient fingers of God. God will accept nothing but the best for His children; remember this. Difficulties, trials and troubles in our lives are there for a purpose and the end result will be good. Yes, we may have to die but the fruit from our lives in this world will reap a great crop. This earth is "temporary" heaven is "eternal"; this life is fleeting, but eternity is secure and permanent.

"My brothers, count it all joy when you fall into various trials, knowing that the testing of your faith produces patience. But let patience have its perfect work, that you may be perfect and complete, lacking nothing." **Vs. 2 & 3**

Patience means to endure or to wait, patience is filled to the top and running over with waiting. I do not like to wait; I want things done now. I think this is sadly true of most people. A person cannot become proficient in anything unless the endure the training that is required to be proficient and excellent in anything. If there was not need for trial and testing everyone would be perfect but we are not perfect we are imperfect or flawed.

In **Romans 8:28** we read that all things work "together" for the good of the believer or those who love God and are called into a specific ministry. But we also read that it is tribulation that must be present in our lives in order to develop patience in our lives. **Romans 5:3** It also tells us that patience brings about experience and with experience we gain hope. Our Hope is in Christ Jesus and that Hope does not disappoint. This hope is an anchor to our lives that can be relied upon. **Hebrews 6:19**

The believer is encouraged here to endure through the struggle with the knowledge that God is in control and therefore let God do His work in our lives and through our lives. Trust God! This trust will bring about peace, God's peace that passes all understanding. **Philippians 4:7** *"And the peace of God, which surpasses all understanding, will guard your hearts and minds through Christ Jesus."* **NKJV**

If we trust God we will live a peaceful and contented life that will be short of nothing at all. *"And my God shall supply all your need according to His riches in glory by Christ Jesus our Lord."* **Philippians 4:19 NKJV**

"If any of you lack wisdom, let him ask of God, who give to all liberally and with out reproach, and it will be given to him. But let him ask in faith, with no doubting, for he who doubts is like a wave of the sea driven and tossed by the wind. For let not that man suppose that he will receive anything from the Lord; he is a double-minded man, unstable in all his ways." **Vs. 5 – 8**

Who among us lacks wisdom? All of us lack wisdom. We are incapable of making decisions in life without the leadership and wisdom of the Holy Spirit. The Holy Spirit was sent from God to be our teacher, our guide and our comfort. In all that the believer does he must first as guidance and understanding from the Holy Spirit. We can only do all things "through" Christ Jesus our Lord.

So, with the understanding that we need wisdom, we need to ask for it from God. Having asked God will then give us the wisdom that we need for the situation and the time slot where we find ourselves. There is no need to question as to whether God will answer; He will answer our request. God is not a respecter of persons although we are in many cases. God is faithful to us; He is with us and He is for us. God's desire is for us to "do His will" and He will empower us to accomplish that mission in life.

So here is the bottom line: When we ask for wisdom, use that wisdom. If you were uncertain of what way to go or what to do; do the thing that God places in your mind after you pray and allow God to work. He "will give guidance" not might or could if He happens to feel an inclination. Ask, trust God and make the decision; don't hesitate but act in confidence of your trust in God. Let your faith be strong at all times. Never be "wishy-washy"; never be as the waves of the sea going this way then that. This hesitation is actually doubting that God will do what He has promised to do. This type of a person should not expect God to him help because he doesn't believe God. This type of a person is "unstable" in every area of his life. This unstable believer must work upon his reliance upon God; he has need of revival and refreshment in his Christian life.

"Let the lowly brother glory in his exaltation, but the rich in his humiliation, because as a flower of the field he will pass away. For no sooner has the sun risen with a burning heart than it withers the grass; its flower falls, and its beautiful appearance perishes. So, the rich man also will fade away in his pursuits." **Vs. 9 – 11**

There is no place in the life of a believer for a haughty and self-sufficient spirit. Again, the success of the ministry of a believer comes only from the work of the Holy Spirit in their life. When God does mighty works in our lives, we cannot boast about it because it could not have been done if we did not have the power of the Holy Spirit working in our lives.

The pattern and caution is this: If you think you can't do nothing, you are right because it is God Who works in us giving us the ability to do what He calls us to do, so, you give Him glory for using you to do wonderful things. Yes, you may be surprised and it also surprises others; and therefore, God receives the glory. As God is glorified, you are exalted as well.

One of the most difficult missions for the believer is in the use of wealth in this world. Aa a person of means, power and ability you have a problem, and the problem is pride in the very riches, means and personal abilities that you have. For God to use a humanly "gifted" person or a person of means, he must show humility by acknowledging that he only possesses these gifts only because of the awesome and good hand of God in His mercy and grace has trusted them with him. That gifted person must be constantly aware that the earthly possessions and abilities cannot be trusted or relied upon but God can, and God can use him. God alone is a sure thing, He alone is faithful and the believer must seek to be faithful with what God has given him.

James is not saying that God cannot use those special gifts that you have been blessed with but he is saying, don't give glory to them but instead give glory to God and God will allow you to use those abilities in His power to do the things that go beyond even those abilities. Be humble; never think you are better than another. We are all children of God and gifted of God.

For anyone to be used of God and successful in accomplishing God's call he must first become nothing in his own eyes. These earthly gifts and possessions will fade but that which is stored in heaven will never fade. *"Do not lay up for yourselves treasures on earth, where moth and rust destroy and where thieves break in and steal but lay up for yourselves treasures in heaven, where neither moth nor rust destroys and where thieves do not break in and steal. For where your treasure is, there will be your heart also."* **Matthew 6:19 – 21 NKJV**

Thank God for all that you have and acknowledge His work and your gifts as from Him alone. This will guarantee success in ministry and life.

"Blessed is the man who endure temptation; for when he has been approved, he will receive the crown of life which the Lord has promised to those who love Him." **Vs. 12**

James tells the reader to count it joy when you experience trials; he tells the reader to ask for wisdom in trials and decision from God; he tells the reader not to place trust in your personal abilities in doing what God has for you in your life and to recognize that what you have came from Him and what you lack will be supplied by Him. Now he add to the joyful spirit of going through not only trials but even in temptations to understand that these are times of strengthening for you. When it is completed you will find that you have been rewarded for those times with a crown of life that God has promised. Nothing can hinder God from achieving His purposes in life, everything that happens to us has been know by God even before the foundations of the earth. Nothing ever just "occurs" to God! God knows "all things"; there was never a time that He did not know them. I can't understand that because that is a "Creator God" thing and I am a "creation" of His and so are you.

"Let no one say when he is tempted, 'I am tempted by God'; for God cannot be tempted by evil, nor does He Himself tempt anyone. But each one is tempted when he is drawn away by his own desires and enticed. Then, when desire has conceived, it gives birth to sin; and sin, when it is full-grown, brings forth death. Do not be deceived, my beloved brethren." **Vs. 13 – 16**

Have you ever said: "Why did God do this?" when something bad happens? Many of the things that happen in our lives, happen because of the fact that we are living in a world that is controlled by Satan and his angels. Our fight is with the principalities and powers of this world and not people. **Ephesians 6:11 & 12** *"Put on the whole armor of God, that you may be able to stand against the wiles of the devil. For we do not wrestle against flesh and blood but against principalities, against powers, against the rulers of the darkness in the heavenly places."* **NKJV**

When man sinned, the whole earth was affected by his sin and when Jesus comes again he will reclaim the deed to this earth and all creation. When He comes he will set up His Kingdom and judge everyone and everything and bring a new Heaven and a new earth with a New Jerusalem as it's city of worship. **2 Peter 3:10 – 13; 1 Chronicles 16:33; Revelation 21:1 & 2**

We live in a world of sin and bad things happen because of sin, and Jesus came to conquer sin. Remember, Jesus has come to save those people upon this earth from the power of sin, not to destroy people. Jesus is the hope of the world. Sin has already condemned mankind, we are already condemned and Jesus came to redeem and save. **John 3:17** *"For God did not send His Son into the world to condemn the world, but that the world through Him might be saved."* **NKJV**

Satan is the tempter, and he comes to entice to do evil. We read of his temptation of Jesus in **Matthew 4:1 – 11**. God does test, try and prove individuals to make them better. Tribulations that happen in our lives are there to develop patience and strength in a person. But God does not tempt to sin, but He will test to prove and to encourage to do better.

Therefore, do not accuse God for the temptations to sin in your life because God cannot sin neither does He tempt anyone. God does God things only. When temptations come God will with the temptation make a way in which we can overcome that temptation. **1 Corinthians 10:13** *"No temptation has overtaken you except such as is common to man; but God is faithful, who will not allow you to be tempted beyond what you are able, but will with the temptation will also make a way of escape, that you may be able to bear it."*

The shield of faith and the armor of God are also means of escape. **Ephesians 6:11 & 12**

So, how and where does temptations come? *"But each one is tempted when he is drawn away by his own desires and enticed"* **VS. 14 The** first step is being drawn away from God by our own desires and then enticed to sin. **James 4:7 & 8** tells us that when we are drawn away by Satan we should resist him. How? By drawing near to God rather than being drawing near to our desires. Our desires ought to be the desires of God not our sinful human nature.

Paul writes of this battle in **Romans 7:13 – 25** *"... For I delight in the law of God according to the inward man. But I see another law in my members, warring against the law of my mind, and baring me into captivity to the law of sin which is in my members..."* **NKJV** and in **Galatians 5:17** *"For the flesh lusts against the Spirit, and the Spirit against the flesh; and these are contrary to one another, so you cannot do the things you wish."* **NKJV**

We are lured away and enticed away from God by the power of sin to do what is natural not spiritual and God's desires. This battle is a daily one and must be waged with the power of the Holy Spirit in our lives. So, resist and draw near to God for the victory against sin. As we draw near God, he draws near us and Satan flees. **James 4:8** The draw to sin gives birth to sin and then having sinned, sin brings death for *"The wages of sin is death.'* **Romans 6:23** Don't fall for the lie of Satan!

"Every good gift and every perfect gift is from above, and comes down from the Father of lights, with whom there is no variation or shadow of turning. Of His own will He brought us forth by the word of truth, that we might be a kind of firstfruits of His creatures." **Vs. 17 & 18**

God is good and He cannot be anything less. Good gifts then come from God. God's gifts are clearly good and totally free of decay or fall short of His expectation in giving them. God's gifts are perfect, they have no flaw in them; they are completely good through and through and they do not change; they also produce more gifts or they bear more fruit of the Spirit. **Galatians 5:22 & 23**

We can be certain that equipped with God's gifts and working in His will, we will always be a display the goodness of God. We are the choice possessions of God and in us He chooses to display His good pleasure to the world. We are His fruit, which reflect His goodness, power and glory to the world.

"So then, my beloved brethren, let every man be swift to hear, slow to speak, slow to wrath; for the wrath of man does not produce the righteousness of God." **Vs. 19 & 20**

Have you ever jumped to a conclusion and the conclusion that you came to was totally wrong? I'm sure you have. Why did this take place? It happened because you were not patient enough to wait or you did not take the time to think through what was happening and you just reacted and that reaction was wrong. James tell his readers to be slow to speak; take time to think. Doing things right is what is important not rushing to get things done.

James also encourages the reader to be slow in turning to wrath for what seems to be wrong at the moment. Even if it is wrong we should not desire to be judge, jury and executioner. Jesus came to redeem and to forgive, so we should be willing to forgive others and restore any broken fellowship with others. It could be that we are the one wrong. Grace and mercy is what the Good News is all about. God is the only good and righteous judge. **2 Timothy 4:8**

When we try to do the work of God we step out of line. We are not called to make this world right, Jesus came and overcame the world and has chosen us to take that gift of righteousness to the world so that they might be saved not punished. It is easy to think judgment thoughts when we see evil but those thoughts will not bring about righteousness they will bring judgment.

Again our fight is not against people but it is against the powers and workers of evil in heavenly places. We bring the opportunity of being made new to the people of this world. Our wrath will only create problems in our lives as well as in the lives of others. The chosen arm of God to execute His wrath and to avenge for evil on this earth are rulers and governing authorities. *"For he is God's minister to you for good. But if you do evil, be afraid; for he does not bear the sword in vain; for he is God's minister, and avenger to execute wrath on him who practices evil."* **Romans 13:4 NKJV**

"Therefore lay aside all filthiness and overflow of wickedness, and receive with meekness the implanted word, which is able to save your souls." **VS. 19 & 20**

Put away everything but that which God has given you and called you to do. He has called the believer to do His will, carry his Gospel and reflect His love to all people. The way the world knows believers is by their love for God is love. **1 John 4:8**

The believer is to be meek but meek is not weak, meekness is power under control doing what is right. The believer is to be gracious, "giving" to others what they do not deserve, good and righteous things. The believer is to be merciful, "not giving" to others what they deserve which is judgment and punishment. The believer is to do good at all times and it is the kindness and goodness of God that leads to repentance. **Romans 2:4** *"Or do you despise the riches of His goodness,* *forbearance, and longsuffering, not knowing that the goodness of God leads you to repentance?* **NKJV**

"But be doers of the word, and not hearers only, deceiving yourselves. For if anyone is a hearer of the word and not a doer, he is like a man observing his natural face in a mirror; for he observes himself, goes away, and immediately forgets what kind of man he was. But he who looks into the perfect law of liberty and continues in it, and is not a forgetful hearer, but a doer of the work, this one will be blessed in what he does." **Vs. 22 – 25**

What you know is not as important as what you do. If you do not do what you know to do then you are living a lie you are deceiving yourself. You know to do better but you choose not to do what you know. James asks that we be doers of the word and not just hearers.

The example of looking into a mirror and forgetting what he has just observed; James is suggesting that if you forget what you have observed, what the purpose of looking in the first place was. The reason one looks into a mirror is to see if there is something that needs to be done, to see how others are observing you. If you see something that need to be corrected, correct it. The purpose for looking into the "perfect" law of liberty is to a line to what you see and read. If we do this then we will be blessed of God in accomplishing that which He has called us to do.

"If anyone among you thinks he is religious, and does not bridle his tongue but deceives his own heart, this one's religion is useless. Pure and undefiled religion before God and the Father is this: 'to visit orphans and widows in their

trouble, and to keep oneself unspotted from the world." **Vs. 26 & 27**

One thing a believer must do is to keep his tongue for spewing out things that are not of God or honoring to God; things that are evil.   The perfect word gives us examples of how to think and what to think. We are to think about things that are pure and   **Philippians 4:8** *"Finally, brethren, whatever things are true, whatever things are noble, whatever things just, what ever things are pure, whatever things are lovely, whatever things are of good report, if there is any virtue and if there is anything praiseworthy –meditate on these things."* **NKJV**

Christianity is not a religion it is a faith, it is a faith in Christ Jesus, it is a living of life that is reflective of Jesus and doing that which He has called us to do. One of the main things a believer must learn to do is to bridle his tongue so he is not saying what he desires to say but what God has given and commanded him to say and to do.

To do anything other than God's desire is useless and worthless in the eyes of God. Christianity is "doing" not just listening and hearing; Christianity is doing what you have heard. What we are called to do is God's will and sharing that Good News with others.   Christianity is making disciple who will in turn make disciple.

The religious part is caring for those who cannot care for themselves and as we do that others see the hand of Jesus through us. Visit the orphans, the widows and the misfortunate that are about us. When we do for other we are less likely not to be drawn away from God to sin.

Chapter 2

"My brethren, do not hold the faith of our Lord Jesus Christ, the Lord of glory, with partiality." **Vs. 1**

God does not show partiality we read in **1:5**. If God is not show partiality then neither should we. The Gnostics of the day, showed partiality by the secret knowledge that they believed God had given to some and not to others. To show special honor to some, then is to dishonor God. How can a true believer dishonor and deny the very God of glory by holding back and keeping the whole Truth from some selected people? This cannot be done; Jesus came for whosoever believes.

"For if there should come into your assembly a man with gold rings, in fine apparel, and there should also come in a poor man in filthy clothes, and you pay attention to the one wearing the fine clothes and say to him, 'You sit here in a good place,' and say to the poor man, 'You stand there,' or 'Sit here at my footstool.' Have you not shown partiality among yourselves, and become judges with evil thoughts? Listen, my beloved brethren: Has God not chosen the poor of this world to be rich in faith and heirs of the kingdom which He promised to those who love Him? But you have dishonored the poor man. Do not the rich oppress you and drag you into the courts? Do they blaspheme that noble name by which you are called? If you really fulfill the royal law according to the Scripture, You shall love your neighbor as yourself, you do well; but if you show partiality, you commit sin, and are convicted by the law as transgressors." **Vs. 2 – 9**

Be careful how you view others. Because someone does not meet up with the expectations that you have or have been taught does not mean they are less worthy of being with you or especially worshiping with you. Jesus had problems with the "religious leaders" of His day. It was the priest, Pharisee, lawyers and scribes of the Law that were revoked by the daily actions and associations of Jesus. He was known to be a friend of sinners. **Luke 7:34** *"So the Son of man has come eating and drinking, and you say, 'Look, a glutton and a winebibber, a friend of tax collectors and sinners!"* **NKJV**

So too, the believer ought to be known as a friend of sinners, in order to win them to our Faith. The believer should desire to be around the sinners and misfits of this world, did not Jesus ask us to take the Gospel to the "whole world'? It is the natural tendency of mankind to stand in awe of those of position and means. The mere use of the word "position" speaks volumes. The place of prominence is to be given to God and to God alone. Everyone else is on level ground and we ought to acknowledge and admit it.

I have had to make a correction in my attitude at times when a person of the street and misfit entered the sanctuary. My first response has often been: "O, I know what they are here for." And I may have been right but it doesn't matter; we have the Good News. We have the Good New to carry to those who do not know of it or do not have a correct understanding of it. The correct attitude ought to have been: "Thank you Lord for sending them here, help be to be faithful in sharing and demonstrating the Good New to them."

In the same light, it is just as shameful for me to feel insufficient or to be resentful and envious of a person of position and wealth and not be quick to present to them the Gospel to that person of means who comes into the sanctuary. They too need the Good News and I ought to be faithful in sharing it with them as well.

Never feel insufficient in presenting the Good News to anyone nor should one feel too good to share that same Good News to the lowest individuals in life. Just carry and share the Good News and do not keep it to yourself or show favoritism.

Generally speaking, it is those of means who resist the spreading of the Gospel because of the means that God has allowed them to gain. It is not the lowly who resist the Gospel; it is the rich.

The thing that the believer ought to take carefully note is, if we show partiality and restrain our love to others; then we sin and are guilty of breaking the whole Law of God. Remember, it was Jesus Who condensed the Law in two statements: *"Jesus said to him, 'You shall love the Lord your God with all your heart, with all your soul, and with all your mind. This is the great commandment. And the second is like it: 'You shall love your neighbor as yourself.' On these two commandments hang all the Law and the Prophets.'"* **Matthew 22;37 – 40 NKJV** Jesus added His commandment to this and it is to love one another as He loved us. *"This is My commandment, that you love one another as I have love you."* **John 15:12 NKJV**

To show favoritism to someone is to break the Commandment of Jesus, which is, to take the Gospel to "The whole world" or to "all" without exception. People recognize a believer by the love that they have and express. *"By this all will know that you are My disciples, if you have love for one another."* **John 13:35 NKJV** Showing favoritism tarnishes the glory of God in the eyes of others and in the eyes of God. This is sin.

"For whoever shall keep the whole law, and yet stumble in one point, he is guilty of all. For He who said, 'Do not commit adultery, also said, 'Do not murder.' Now if you do not commit adultery, but you do murder, you have become a transgressor of the law, so speak and so do as those who will be judged by the law of liberty. For judgment is without mercy to the one who has shown no mercy. Mercy triumphs over judgment." **Vs. 11 – 13**

The unrighteous believer is judged by the righteousness of Jesus and for that we should always be mindful and thankful. (**2 Corinthians 5:21**) It is not by our righteousness that we have eternal life but the righteousness of Jesus. *"There is none righteous, no, not one."* **Romans 3:10** The only one who is good and righteous is Jesus. **Luke 18:19**

But the believer still must strive to be "like Jesus" and Jesus is pure and holy; so we are to strive to be pure and holy just as He is. **1 Peter 1:13 – 16 NKJV** *"Therefore gird up the loins of your mind, be sober, and rest your hope fully upon the grace that is to be brought to you a the revelation of Jesus Christ; as obedient children, not conforming yourselves to the former lusts, a in your ignorance; but as He who called you is holy, you also be holy in all your conduct, because it is written: 'Be holy, for I am holy.' "*

All Scripture, we read in **2 Timothy 3:16**, is given to us to guide us and to correct us in our daily living. A believer can be recognized by the love in which he adheres to and his applying the love of Christ to his life and expressing that love into the lives of others. The believer must keep this commandment of Jesus at all times. This love of Jesus carries with it His great gift of eternal life. Never forget, because we are forgiven and have been set free of the penalty of sin does not mean we can live as we wish, it means that we have a responsibility to carry the Good News and live like Jesus. It is not a get out of jail free card it is a how to live card; even if you are in jail. Stay in love with Jesus, continue to share His Gospel and live a life that reflects Jesus. Keep your life free from sin. It's all about Him and them.

An interesting phrase is *"Mercy triumphs over judgment."* **Vs. 13 What** does that mean? How does mercy triumph over judgment? God tells us that He shows mercy to whomever He wishes. **Romans 9:15**

God is saying that it is His judgment to show mercy to whomever He wishes on the basis that He is sovereign over all. God is above all and on that Truth and fact He displays mercy. Mercy is not giving to someone what they deserve. We deserve hell because of our sin but God triumphs or overrides the judgment by His indisputable mercy. God says: NO! Though the accuser, Satan says guilty, God says: "Yes, the Law does say guilty but I say there is no sin. For I have made this sin to be "no sin" **2 Corinthians 5:21** How can that be? Because God says it is so; end of discussion.

Now that is a powerful statement and a powerful reason to obey God. What has happened is God has justified the ungodly by making them to have the righteousness of God. **Romans 4:5; 2 Corinthians 5:21**

"What does it profit, my brethren, if someone says he has faith but does not have works? Can faith save him? If a brother or sister is naked and destitute of daily food, and one of you says to them, 'Depart in peace, be warmed and filled.' But you do not give them the things which are needed for the body, what does it profit? Thus also faith by itself, if it does not have works is dead. But someone will say, 'You have faith, and I have works.' Show me your faith without your works, and I will show you my faith by my works. You believe that there is one God. You do well. Even the devils believe-and tremble! But do you want to know, O foolish man, that faith without works is dead? Was not Abraham our father justified by works when he offered Isaac his son on the altar? Do you see that faith was working together with his works, and by works faith was made perfect? And the Scripture was fulfilled which says, 'Abraham believed God, and it was accounted to him for righteousness.' And he was called the friend of God. You see then that a man is justified by works, and not by faith only. Likewise, was not Rahab the harlot also justified by works when she received the messengers and sent them out another way? For as the body without the spirit is dead, so faith without works I dead also. **Vs. 14 - 26**

Faith without works is dead in the same way as having knowledge and not using the knowledge that you have. What good is knowledge without putting it to work? If a doctor has the knowledge to heal a sick person of the disease that they have but does not use that knowledge to bring about healing; what good is that knowledge benefiting here?   He might as well not have the knowledge. Ignorance is as beneficial here as unused knowledge. His knowledge is useless. So, that type of faith, without the needed and applied works is dead or of no value. That type of faith is dead-faith.

Can workless faith save? No, it cannot. The truth is you have no faith if you do not apply works with it; faith requires works. Works do not save but the works that one has reveals his faith; it gives credibility to faith as being a genuine faith.

Jesus tells us that "whosoever believes in Him has everlasting life." **John 3:16 But** to believe is to have genuine, belief, trust and faith. Even the devils believe that Jesus is the Son of God and shutter in fear of their belief. But, what they know will not save them; they do not have saving faith their works reveal their master, Satan. God will have no mercy upon them.   A "step of faith" is a work of faith and that is what is required to become a believer in Christ Jesus.

Examples of faith with works are given here:

Abraham: He believed and the expression of his belief and faith was to place
                Isaac on the altar. His works revealed his faith in God as genuine.
                Abraham was called a friend of God.

Rehab: She believed the messengers as from God and her actions brought to her
                salvation.

The body: The body without the spirit is dead and so faith without works is dead
                faith.

Chapter 3

"My brethren, let not many of you become teachers, knowing that we shall receive a stricter judgment." **Vs. 1**

Jesus says in **Luke 12:48b** *". . . For everyone to whom much is given, from him much will be required; and to whom much has been committed, of him they will ask the more."* **NKJV**

It is The Holy Spirit Who calls one to a specific mission or a specific calling in life. Whatever God calls us to do He requires us to do that and if we fall short then we will be judged and judged more severely that those who have not been given that responsibility. This is a warning to do well and with excellence that which God has called us to do. God has committed to us a special mission and we do not want to be found unfaithful in that task; as a shepherd is given responsibility to a specific flock to care for so the called of God is given a special responsibility. Not to carefully fulfill that responsibility carries with it a severe punishment. Luke writes in the book of **Acts:** *"Therefore take heed to yourselves and to all the flock, among which the Holy Spirit has made you overseers, to shepherd the church of God which He purchased with His own blood."* **Acts 20:28** The believer is not to "seek" for himself a position of leadership and teaching but must be called of the Lord. The responsibility is great in that there will be many false teachers who will come in to destroy the lives of many believers. The called must be vigilant to fulfill that calling of God and to protect God's church and to arm His people. This is a great calling and awesome in responsibility. There is nothing greater than to be called to do for God. *"But none of these things move me; nor do I count my life dear to myself, so that I may finish my race with joy, and the ministry which I received from the Lord Jesus to testify to the gospel of the grace of God."* **Acts 20:24** The Lord not only calls but He is also the one who supplies and equips those whom He has called as well. (*And my God shall supply all your need according to His riches in glory by Christ Jesus.*) **Philippians 4:23**

A teacher, a preacher or a called one to carry out a God given responsibility is so much greater than any other personal ambition. The call carries with it a greater than ordinary obligation in the way in which that person conducts himself; he must live a life that is *"beyond reproach"* and *"he must have a good testimony among those who are outside, lest he fall into reproach and the snare of the devil."* **1 Timothy 3:2 & 7 NKJV**

No one but God calls, no other person, no other experience can do what God alone desires to do. So, James is saying that no one should have as there ambition to be a leader, a teacher or preacher but rather that ambition ought to be to do whatever God alone calls him to do. If we follow God and not our own desires or the desire of someone else, we will be fully successful in life, happy in life, productive in and live a God pleasing and rewarding life. Seek to do "His Will" not our will.

"For we all stumble in many thing. If anyone does not stumble in word, he is a perfect man able also to bridle the whole body. Indeed, we put bits in the horses' mouths that

they may obey us, and we turn their whole body. Look also at ships: although they are so large and are driven by fierce winds, they are turned by a very small rudder wherever the pilot desires. Even so the tongue is a little member and boasts great things. See how great a forest a little fire kindles! And the tongue is a fire, a world of iniquity. The tongue is so set among our members that it defiles the whole body, and sets on fire the course of nature; and it is set on fire by hell. For every kind of beast and bird of reptile and creature of the sea, is tamed and has been tamed by mankind. But no man can tame the tongue. It is an unruly evil, full of deadly poison. With it we bless our God and Father, and with it we curse men, who have been made in the similitude of God. Out of the same mouth proceeds blessing and cursing. My brethren, these things ought not to be so. Does a spring send forth fresh water and bitter from the same opening? Can a fig tree, my brethren, bear olives or a grapevine bear figs? Thus no spring yields both salt water and fresh." **Vss. 2 - 12**

Stumbling is a human thing and as human we all stumble, if we didn't we would not be human we would be perfect as God is perfect. Since we are human, we must understand that we will falter, stumble or veer from our aim from time to time. One of the greatest problems as human beings is our tongue. The tongue can inspire, and challenge or discourage and hinder. The tongue, though created by God, can be used by Satan to do his will other than the will of God. Small things, designed to do great things can do amazing things, unbelievable things. Never think that you are too small to do that with which God has called you to do. But never allow that small thing within you, your tongue, to cause you not to do those things that God has called you to do. Strive to overcome it, bridle it; do not allow it to bridle you. Never feel that you are beyond the control of your tongue, *"Therefore let him who thinks he stands take heed lest he fall."* **1 Corinthians 10:12 NKJV** *"Finally, my brethren, be strong in the Lord and in the power of His might."* **Ephesians 6:10 NKJV**

Use your tongue to do mighty things for God not mighty things for Satan. Though you may have great storms in life, resist them with what God has given you. Give fresh and cool cups of water not cups filled with salt and bitterness.

"Who is wise and understanding among you? Let him show by good conduct that his works are done in the meekness of wisdom. But if you have bitter envy and self seeking in your hearts, do not boast and lie against the truth. This wisdom that is from above is first pure, then peaceable, gentle, willing to yield, full of mercy and good fruits, without partiality and without hypocrisy. Now the fruit of righteousness is sown in peace by those who make peace." **Vss. 13 – 18**

Seek knowledge, seek wisdom but with all our seeking get understanding. *"Wisdom is the principle thing; Therefore get wisdom, and in all your getting; get understanding."* **Proverbs 4:7 NKJV**

A wise person is a person is one who not only has information but displays what he knows through wise actions. A wise person understands and having understanding, his life reflects it by his conduct. A wise person is not haughty, he is meek. A meek person is not a weak person but possesses strength but bridles that power and directs his paths in the ways of God, not anything other way. He knows, he speaks, he is humble and he is able to relay that wisdom to others, he is able to teach and instruct others and others desire to be trained by him.

A wise person and teacher does not want what God has given to others, he wants to give to others. A wise person sees his place in life as doing what God has called him to do and he focuses his eyes on others to help them. A wise person sees life in a two-fold vision: It's all about Him and them. Love the Lord your God with all your heart and your neighbor as yourself. There is no bitter bone in his body.

A wise person is real, he is as he is seen to be. The thoughts and intents of his heart are all about God and so his mouth speaks those things.

The words used here speak for themselves:
- Pure: Untainted
- Peaceable: Contented
- Gentle: Approachable
- Yielding: Listens and will move as God moves him.
- Merciful: He does not give others what they deserve.
- Fruitful in righteousness: Life is full of the fruits of the Spirit
- Non-partial: Does not show favoritism.
- Genuine: Always the same.
- Sows the seed of peace and produces peace: Leaves peace wherever he goes.

Chapter 4

"Where do wars and fights come from among you? Do they not come from your desires for pleasure that war in your members? **Vs. 1**

Have you ever wondered why fights break out and wars come about? Peter answers the question for us here: They happen when we do not sow the fruits of the Sprit but throw around our desire to do what we want to do and if anyone might get in our way, then we label them as "our enemy". They come about because of selfishness and because these warriors do not possess the wisdom of God nor the fruits of the Spirit. What is in play here is the *"works of the flesh".* **Galatians 5:17 – 21**

"You lust and do not have. You murder and covet and cannot obtain. You fight and war. Yet you do not have because you do not ask. You ask and do not receive, because you ask amiss, that you may spend it on your pleasures. Adulterers and adulteresses! Do you not know that friendship with the world is enmity with God? Whoever therefore wants to be a friend of the world make himself an enemy of God. Or do you thing that the Scripture says in vain,' the Sprit who dwells in us yearns jealously'? But He gives more grace. Therefore, He says: 'God resist the proud, but he gives grace to the humble.'" **Vss. 2 - 6**

Wars come because we have a greater desire to do our will rather than the will of God. Our passion, our obsession and our ambition in life is not pure and holy or magnificent and glorious in God's eyes but in our eyes. Therefore, we war and fight and we also do not have our prayers answered because of that selfish and worldly mindset. Our eyes are not on God and His mission but inward and personal. We see the world and the things that are in it and we want them more than we want the approval of God. We redefine God's will as inline with our will. What we ask of God is not things that are pleasing to him but to us. We want things so we can enjoy them. We want fellowship with others more than we desire the fellowship with God.

God is a jealous God and He cannot share a divided loyalty. James says here that we are *"friends of the world"*. God is pure and holy and the world is defiled with sin and selfishness. How can we expect God to answer our prayers if we seek things that are opposite and contrary to God? *"The Spirit who dwells in us yearns jealously."*

God does give grace but He does not give His grace to self seeking and those who are full of themselves and not full of God. God pours out his grace upon the humble.

"Therefore submit to God. Resist the devil and he will flee from you. Draw near to God and He will draw near to you. Cleanse your hands you sinners and purify your hearts, you double-minded. Lament and mourn and weep! Let your laughter be turned to mourning and your joy to gloom. Humble yourselves in the sight of the Lord, and he will lift you up." **Vs. 7 - 10**

You can stop the wars in your life by submitting to God and resisting the pull of the devil in your life. You resist the devil by drawing near to God. Satan will not be where God is. As you make the first step of turning to God, drawing nearer to Him He in turn draws near to you.

In order to turn or draw near God means that you must realize that you have sin in your life and you need to get rid of that sin. You must stop being around the bad influence in your life and seek the fellowship of those who are pure hearted. As James mentions in **1:5 – 8** Ask God for wisdom and don't be "wishie-washie" or uncertain in what to do, do what you know you must do and do it quickly.

A right attitude must be in place here and that is you are honestly sorrowful for what you have done and grieving in your spirit for not listening to the Spirit in your life. If you are "*humble*", genuinely sorrowful, then God will give you that true joy once again and he will lift you up in your spirit.

"Do not speak evil of one another, brethren. He who speaks evil of a brother and judges his brother, speaks evil of the law and judges the law. But if you judge the law, you are not a doer of the law but a judge. There is one Lawgiver, who is able to save and to destroy. Who are you t judge another?" **VS. 11 & 12**

It is a difficult thing not to judge the actions of others. The truth of the matter is that what we think we see is not the whole story. God is the only one who knows the thoughts and intents of the heart and can judge them. He not only knows them but He knew them before the foundations of the world. Scripture can help us discern the thoughts and intents of the heart. **Hebrews 4:12** With this understanding we must resist the desire to judge and fix our mind upon ourselves to be more like Christ and seek to be encouragers and helpers to others to do what which God has called them to do and edify others. The Holy Spirit is the One Who convicts of sin and we are the carrier of the Gospel.

Hebrews 10:31 tells us that *"it is a fearful thing to fall into the hands of a living God,".* We have a difficult enough time keeping ourselves in line with the Word of God to spend any time judging the actions and intentions of others.

"Come now, you who say, 'Today or tomorrow we will go to such and such a city, spend a year there, buy and sell, and make a profit'; whereas you do not know what will happen tomorrow. For what is your life? It is even a vapor that appears for a little time and then vanishes away. Instead you ought to say, 'If the Lord wills, we shall live and o this or that.' But now you boast in your arrogance. All such boasting is evil. Therefore, to him who knows to do good and does not do it, to him it is sin." **Vs. 13 – 17**

Did you know that we all live in a fog? Well, we actually do. We live in a fog because we have no idea what is or will be before us. All our careful planning cannot predict what we will face in the near or distant future. How then shall we live? We live in the fear of the Lord and in the care of the Lord. We live our lives doing what He may place before us. We prepare ourselves to become knowledgeable and wise servants of the Lord and we strive to be diligent in all that we are given to do but we leave the future in the hands of the One who knows all things. We need to have a plan and we need to work that plan but we must leave the directing of our lives in the capable hands of an all knowing, all sufficient, ever present, all powerful and unchanging God. He is our hope and all our trust and faith is in Him and in Him alone. Our plans, however great they may seem to be, are not secure but we are secure in Him and His will is secure. Never boast about what God has done in your life, rather, give Him the glory in which belongs to Him.

We all stand on level ground before God and no one is greater in Gods eyes than another. Jesus tells us that if we do not come to Him and serve him as little children then we cannot enter the kingdom of God. **Luke 18:17** *"Assuredly, I say to you, whoever does not receive the kingdom of God as a little child will by no means enter it."* **NKJV**

God calls us, God supplies us, God protects us and God leads us. We can depend upon this but we can in no way can we depend upon ourselves; or the sufficiency of any other.

Our aim is to seek to do God's good will and to do it with all our might and in the power of His might. If we know His will in our lives and we understand that it is He who has called us to a mission and we do not do it, then not doing it is sin. We sin by omission.

Chapter 5

"Come, now, you rich, weep and howl for your miseries that are coming upon you! Your riches are corrupt, and your garments are moth-eaten. Your gold and silver are corroded, and their corrosion will be a witness against you and will eat your flesh like fire. You have heaped up treasure in the last days. Indeed the wages of the laborers who mowed your fields, which you kept back by fraud, cry out; and the cries of the reapers have reached the ears of the Lord of Sabaoth. You have lived on the earth in pleasure and luxury; you have fattened your hearts as in a day of slaughter. You have condemned, you have murdered the just; he does not resist you." **Vs. 1 – 6**

Riches are not evil but riches can corrupt. Not everyone can be a righteous rich person. Riches are not evil but they are often the source of evil actions as the Apostle Paul warned his protégé Timothy. *"For the love of money is a root of all kinds of evil, for which some have strayed from the faith in their greediness, and pierced themselves through with many sorrows."* **1 Timothy 6:10 NKJV**

Rather than crave the will of God they crave the benefits of riches. Riches can get your eyes fixed upon yourself and off God. There are many preachers of the Gospel who have found themselves trapped in the grip of riches and they become a "fraud" or not the real thing. They confuse people as they see the vast riches they have piled up and perhaps question how these riches came to be.

Jesus suggests that we store up treasures in heaven rather than heap up treasure on earth. *"Do not lay up for yourselves treasures on earth, where moth and rust destroy and where thieves break in and steal; but lay up for yourselves treasures in heaven, where neither moth nor rust destroys and where thieve do not break in and steal. For where you treasure is, there you heart will be also."* **Matthew 6:19 – 21 NKJV**

"Therefore be patient, brethren, until the coming of the Lord. See how the farmer waits for the precious fruit of the earth, waiting patiently for it until it receives the early and later rain. You also be patient. Establish your hearts, for the coming of the Lord is at hand. Do not grumble against one another, brethren, lest you be condemned. Behold, the Judge is standing at the door!" **Vs. 7 - 9**

Patience is not easy and in order to be patient one must also be confident, have hope and faith in what he is waiting upon. For the believer it is the coming of our Lord Jesus. Being patient and having confidence in the Word of the Lord as being true and sure than what we are waiting for is worthy of the wait.

Patiently the believer waits; resisting the ever-present urge to become unhappy with others who are waiting with us. If the believer will read the letters that are written to him his life will be much more pleasant. Remember, in the hour that we think not, the Son of Man will come. Life is short, even as a mist. Look, He is even at the door!

"My brethren, take the prophets, who spoke in the name of the Lord, as an example of suffering and patience. Indeed we count them blessed who endure. You have heard of the perseverance of Job and seen the end intended by the Lord-that the Lord is very compassionate and merciful. But above all, my brethren, do not swear, either by heaven or by earth or with any other oath. But let your 'Yes' be 'Yes', and your 'No, 'No', lest you fall into judgment." **Vs. 10 – 12**

James suggest that we remember that all those prophets who wrote, wrote not having clear understanding of what they were writing because they were writing under the moving of the Holy Spirit. *"knowing this first, that no prophecy of Scripture is of any private interpretation, for prophecy never came by the will of man, but holy men of God spoke as they were moved by the Holy Sprit."* **2 Peter 1:20 – 21 NKJV**

We read Scripture and see the faithful hand of God moving and proving to be faithful and they are evidences for us to remember and to give us the confidence to trust God.

So, in these last times the believer must be patient, he must endure the struggle of our short life; he must see that the reward is worth the wait and struggle. The believer can see revealed in life, what is written in Scripture that all things actually did work out for the good in a gracious and merciful way.

It seems a bit out of place here to bring up the idea of making an oath or swearing but the idea is that people need to believe us on just by the fact that we say it. Our word is our bond, as the saying goes. The integrity of the believer ought to be known as trustworthy by all who know us. If we take an oath, not knowing what might happen in the future we may end up sinning and fall into judgment because of it.

"Is anyone among you suffering? Let him pray. Is any one cheerful? Let him sing psalms. Is anyone among you sick? Let him call for the elders of the church, and let them praying over him, anointing him with oil in the name of the Lord. And the prayer of faith will save the sick, and the Lord will raise him up. And if he has committed sins, he will be forgiven. Confess your trespasses to one another, and pray for one another, that you may be healed. The effective, fervent prayer of a righteous man avails much. Elijah was a man with a nature like ours, and he prayed earnestly that it would not rain; and it did not rain on the land for three years and six months. And he prayed again, and the heaven gave rain, and the earth produced its fruit." **Vs. 13 – 18**

Suffering is not pleasant but the truth is everyone who is born on this earth <u>will</u> suffer from time to time and for various lengths of time. Suffering is tribulation and tribulation is trials and trials produce knowledge of various things and this knowledge gives opportunity to gain understanding and then understanding gives way to wisdom and true wisdom comes from God. *"The fear of the Lord is the beginning of knowledge, but fools despise wisdom and understanding."* **Proverbs 1:7 NKJV** James tells us to "let patience have her perfect work." (**1:4**)

A believer must endure suffering and learn from it. James here says that in the time of suffering we ought to pray for understanding and guidance. If one is not suffering then he must be happy, cheerful and joyful so at these times one ought to sing. Singing is an expression of the soul. Paul writes in **Colossians 3:16** *"Let the word of Christ dwell in you richly in all wisdom, teaching and admonishing one another in psalms and hymns and spiritual songs, singing and with grace in your heart to the Lord."* **NKJV** With a joyful heart we must sing. In our singing we encourage in that we are singing from our heart. *"A merry heart makes a cheerful countenance."* **Proverbs 15:13 NKJV The** Psalms contain many expressions of joy.

Everyone suffers, everyone experiences times of joy and everyone also will find himself in need of healing. God heals. The greatest healing that God has brought to us is the healing of the soul; and this is eternally achieved by the blood of Jesus shed for us and by our repenting of our sin and accepting His gift through faith. We receive in return for our unrighteousness, the righteousness of Jesus as He take our sin upon Himself. This gift is freely given to all who would believe but you cannot have it unless you believe in Him. **John 3:16**

It is also true that God heals the physical body. God healed people in the past; God heals people today and he will continue to heal people until time is no more. But often God does not always choose to heal for reasons that only He knows. God is Sovereign. In these times, God is not to be questioned but trusted in faith. In these times God's purposes are being worked out in our lives and He gives to us is grace that is more than sufficient. **2 Corinthians 12:9** *"And He said to me, 'my grace is sufficient for you, for My strength is made perfect in weakness.' Therefore, most gladly I will rather boast in my infirmities, that the power of Christ may rest upon me."* **NKJV**

Paul prayed three times for a thorn in his life to be taken away; but Paul tells us the answer of God to his prayer was in effect; "The best way for Me to be glorified, in your life is to allow you to have this "thorn". Jesus said the same thing concerning the request of Martha and Mary for him to go to Lazarus immediately, we read in **John 11:4** That this "sickness" which resulted in Lazarus' death was *"that the Son of God might be glorified"*. Being physically healed may not be the best thing in God's eyes.

If we ask in faith and fervently for healing and it does not come, trust God. One thing that we can be certain is that God is good and all that He does is good. Remember these seven things:

1. Sometimes healing is not immediate.
2. Sometimes healing may come but He asks of us to do something.
3. Sometimes healing may be delayed for reasons that are not understood at the time.
4. Sometimes we may have sin in our lives that must be addressed.
5. Sometimes there may be others around us that need to witness our faithfulness in suffering.
6. Sometimes our ministry may include suffering.
7. At all times God's response to our prayer is perfect, loving, kind, gracious and merciful.

Dr. Bill Bright, the founder of Campus Crusade for Christ, who was ravaged by many ailments said of his suffering. *"Nothing can happen to us but that has not first been filtered through the loving fingers of God"*.

If you hurt then pray and get as close to God as you can and allow Him to put His great arms around you and love on you, encourage you and sustain you.

James gives the believer a process for praying for healing:

- Call for the elders of the church. Why? So they can enter into this difficult time with you to encourage and help you and them as well. We need fellowship with strong and faithful people of God.
- Anointing with oil is a symbol of acknowledging God's blessing and moving.
- This prayer will save the sick and the Lord will raise him up.
- He must confess known sins in his life, to be forgiven by the Lord.
- Everyone must confess their sin to each other for purity and holiness.
- This is fervent praying, sincere and effectual praying, it is prayer that makes a difference.

The example of praying that James gives here is that of Elijah. Elijah was an ordinary man but he had extra-ordinary faith and he prayed in an extra-ordinary way, with fervor and his prayers were effective.

One more thing, there are those who exploit believers with their "gift of healing". I will not judge but I will suggest that you "test" the spirits, investigate the life of the one to see if they are of God or not. Are they doing what they do for profit? What does their lives reveal? What does the Holy Spirit say to you? Do not believe every spirit as though they are from God. Do they display the Fruits of the Spirit? You can trust God's Word but you must not trust the word of any individual.

"Brethren, if anyone among you wanders from the truth, and someone turns him back, let him know that he who turns a sinner from the error of his way will save a soul from death and cover a multitude of sins." **Vs. 19 & 20**

The believer has a special mission that he must be diligent in performing and that is to be a watchman for the fellowship of believers. Be alert and if we see a fellow believer straying from the Truth, make every effort to restore the one that is straying and if we are faithful in doing that then we will save that person from a life spent in additional days of sins and perhaps sins that may lead to their death.

Life here on this earth is a life of daily battle against principalities, power and workers of evil in heavenly place. We will be attacked, we will have to suffer, we will have to live periods of time plagued by sickness but God is good and God is kind and He is with us and will never leave us. God gives us understanding, wisdom and grace for each day. He is faithful, so we must strive to be faithful.

Just the Basics
Discovering the Truth in an Untruthful World

Commentary on First Peter

By
Danny Glenn Thomas

Introduction

"The task of the scholar is to guarantee the purity of the text; to get as close as possible to the word as originally given. He may compare Scripture with Scripture until he discovers the true meaning of the text, but right there his authority ends. He must never sit in judgment upon what is written. He must not bring the meaning of the word before the bar of his reason." **A. W. Tozar**

The Epistle of **1 Peter** is written by the Apostle Simon Peter and to the churches who had been dispersed. (**1 Peter 1:1 NKJV** *"Peter, an apostle of Jesus Christ, to the pilgrims of the Dispersion.*)

Peter is writing to these churches to warn them against the impending danger of infiltration by false prophets and false teachers. The early church had many individuals who were trying to sneak in and to carry them away with their false doctrine that denied the authenticity of the Apostles. These false teachers were trying to layer into the doctrine of the Gospel of Jesus many of the tenants of Greek mythology and human intellect.

A second warning was the presence of persecution that they were experiencing and with the warning he desired to encourage them to remain faithful. He desired that they be consistent in their daily living and submission to all elements of life; to live peacefully with all those around them from government, work, family and even slavery. How they lived was the main thing; they were not to rebel but to proclaim the Good News verbally and by their manor of living.

Persecution and suffering were to be expected because our adversary is Satan but the believer is not alone for we have at our side the Holy Spirit who is our strength, and sustainer. **1 Peter 5:9 & 10**

Chapter One:

"Peter, and apostle of Jesus Christ." **1:1 NKJV**

Peter makes himself know to the readers of his letter and he also makes know the authority that he has. He is Peter, the disciple of Jesus Christ who spent three years under His teaching and a half-year with Jesus after His resurrection from the grave and His ascension into heaven. He is that disciple of Christ.

"To the pilgrims of the Dispersion in Pontus, Galatia, Cappadocia, Asia and Bithynia." **1:1 NKJV**

The pilgrims are those believers who had been run out or <u>dispersed</u> (Called the *Diaspora* in Greek) from Jerusalem to other areas. The areas mentioned are states or provinces of the area of what is today Turkey. These people were not citizens of the area but mere travelers and wayfarers traveling through those areas. These believers lived uncertain lives because of the persecution of the government and or the native people of the area. They were shunned, mistrusted and disliked by those that they lived around. Just being able to live a peaceful life was in question. Nero was the Emperor of Rome at the time Peter wrote this letter. (Approximately A.D. 65) Suffering and persecution was just part of everyday life of the early believer.

The believer today finds himself in the same predicament. Today we are just the pilgrim and wayfarer making our way through this world in which we live. People still today question our faith, our way of life and actions in life. How we live is strange to them. It is strange, questioned and misunderstood because it can only be spiritually understood. Our way of life is not learned but revealed to us by our teacher the Holy Spirit. As we live our lives we come to a realization of the power of God and the provisions of God as we obey him in our mission in life. Peter will deal with this later on in his letter.

"Elect according to the foreknowledge of God the Father," **1:2 NJKV**

We are the elect in that God has always known us, we are chosen because of God's *"Foreknowledge".* Foreknowledge is knowing before time or ahead of time. One of the characteristics of God is that He is "all-knowing" or "Omniscient". There is nothing that can be known but what God has always known it and all that can be known of it. There was never a time in eternity that God did not know everything. That is a God thought and there is no way that a created being can understand the mind and thoughts of the Creator in even the most infinitesimal way.

At the point of creation God had already known about me and you completely and in that understanding or foreknowledge of us, God knew the choices we would make. The believer became one of His chosen or to be included in an elite group of creations; that special group is those who would make a free choice to to repent of their sins, believe His Word and trust in God for their redemption from the penalty of sin which is eternal death. In other words, they would take His Only Begotten Son Jesus as their Lord and Savior.

God the Fathers chosen way of redemption was to send His Only Begotten Son to die for our sin and be able to justly forgive our sin by His resurrection from the grave. At that point Jesus conquered sin and the grave and gained the right to forgive all who would believe in Him. **John 3:16** *"For God so loved the world that He Gave His only begotten Son, that whoever believes in Him should not perish but have everlasting life."* **NKJV** God foreknew us and therefore could call us His elect.

"in the sanctification of the Spirit." **Vs. 2**

Sanctification is to be set apart or in light of God, set apart for holiness. The believer, those elect and chosen ones have been therefore by the foreknowledge of the Father made holy and set apart for a holy mission and purpose and the Holy Spirit is the power behind this being set apart.

"for obedience and sprinkling of the blood of Jesus Christ." **Vs. 2 NKJV**

The Father is the planner, the Holy Spirit is the one who has set us apart and made the reservation for ministry and redemption and Jesus Christ the Only begotten Son of God is the one who made the cleansing and righteous sacrifice with His own blood and He is the object of our obedience, He is the one who did the will of the Father and we are those who do the will of the Only Begotten Son, empowered by the Holy Spirit of God. We are those elect, those who have been called to do His will and are to be obedient to His Word.

"Grace to you and peace be multiplied." **NKJV**

Grace is unmerited favor. Grace is undeserved and the Grace of God has been given to those who have believed in Him and taken Him as their personal Lord and Savior. Peace is the peace of God and is not the peace of this world. We have recorded in **John 14:27** where Jesus talks about His peace; He tells us that He leaves peace "with" us. His peace is not something that we have to request, we have His peace because Jesus left it with us. His peace is not the same as worldly peace because worldly peace is fleeting and temporary. God's peace, however, is enduring and it will never leave us because He is ever with us.

He continues by telling us not to be afraid as we go through life or to be troubled in life but rather enjoy His enduring peace throughout life. Jesus is not saying that we won't have trouble, He says that we are to "expect trouble" because that is what is in this troubled world. The believer is a traveler in this world on our way to our home in heaven where we can experience fulfilled and complete peace. Peter here tells the believer that he can expect to come to better understand this peace more and more as we go through life, or as is expressed here in the King James Version, "peace be multiplied" to us.

"Blessed be the God and Father of our Lord Jesus Christ, who according to His abundant mercy has begotten us again to a living hope through the resurrection of Jesus Christ from the dead," **Vs. 3 NKJV**

To be blessed means to be honored, to be envied by others, because of a special favor of God. The **Amplified**

Bible uses the term *Life-joy*; it is having the special good hand of God upon you. But here Peter praises God and desires for God to be blessed by the believer because of what God has done for him. Because God has blessed us in such a marvelous way, Peter gives praise to God for His goodness. This special blessing from God is a team effort of the whole Godhead and that effort has secured for us something that is impossible and that is a right standing before God. *"For with God nothing will be impossible."* **Luke 1:37 NKJV**

Why would God do such a thing? God does it because He wants to do it and if He wants to do something then His desire will be done. God does this by His Grace and Mercy. Grace is giving something that is not deserved and we do not deserve heaven or His blessing but we receive it because of His Grace. Mercy deals with His desire in a different way; mercy is not giving someone what the deserve. Humanity deserves hell because of sin. God is pure and holy and cannot even look upon sin, it was the righteous blood of Jesus that was poured upon our sin that cleansed sin thoroughly. **2 Corinthians 5:21** tells us that God took His Son Jesus who did not even know sin and made Him to actually be sin by becoming a creation; and then poured that precious blood upon the believer and the believer became the righteousness of God because of the righteous blood of Jesus.

On our best day doing the best thing of our whole life does not come anywhere near what God demands of us. It took the blood of His Only Begotten Son to make us acceptable for God's Kingdom. There is nothing that we can do to make our acceptability to God greater than what Jesus has already done. Anything else takes away from His glorious gift. Jesus died for our sin and for His once and only gift we became acceptable to God. *"So, Christ was offered once to bear the sins of many. To those who eagerly wait for Him He will appear a second time, apart from sin for salvation."* **Hebrews 9:28 NKJV;** *"But this Man, after He had offered one sacrifice for sins forever, sat down at the right hand of God from that time waiting for 'til His enemies are made His footstool. For by one offering He has perfected forever those who are being sanctified."* **NKJV Hebrews 10:12 - 14**   Now God extends His mercy to us and revokes our condemnation to hell and by His Grace gives us heaven. That is His abundant mercy. This is why we are called "new creations"; our sins have been voided or we have been made new as though we had never sinned.

Because Jesus is alive, He then is our living hope; our living hope is our living faith and that living faith is anchored in Him. *"This hope we have as an anchor of the soul, both sure and steadfast, and which enters the Presence behind the veil, where the forerunner has entered for us, even Jesus, having become High Priest forever according to the order of Melchiaedek."* **NKJV Hebrews 6;19 & 20**   Yes, Jesus is not dead He is alive! To this thought Peter says: *"Blessed be the God and Father of our Lord Jesus Christ"* **NKJV**

"to an inheritance incorruptible and undefiled and that does not fade away, reserved in heaven for you." **Vs. 4 NKJV**

It is a wonderful thought and truth that Jesus has done all that is necessary to make us acceptable to the Father isn't it. This work is guaranteed to be incorruptible and cannot be changed or altered in anyway by anyone. *"For by one offering He has perfected forever those who are being saved."* **NKJV Hebrews 10:14;** *"Now He who has prepared us for this very thing is God, who also has given us the Spirit as a guarantee."* **NKJV 2 Corinthians 5:5**

This is an *"inheritance"* we have it because we are members of the family of God, we are His children and that does not fade away because we have been "born again" into His family. This inheritance is not collective but an individual reservation it is *"for you"*. God knows you personally because you are His creation and New Creation. You have the righteousness of Jesus poured out upon you.

This reservation is specific for you and specifically in God's Heaven, His New Heaven where He is. As Jesus told the thief on the cross: *"And Jesus said to him, 'Assuredly, I say to you, today you will be with Me in Paradise."* **NKJV Luke 23:43**

"who are kept by the power of God through faith for salvation ready to be revealed in the last time." **NKJV Vs. 5**

Peter adds strength to his statement by saying that we are *"kept"* by the power of God *"through our faith"* and *"for salvation"* . Because of our faith in Christ and the power of His sacrifice that was made for us we can be confident that we will actually receive this promised reward. Our hope will become sight, revealed to us; we will see it personally. Once we enter into our promised homeland in God's newly created Heavens and the earth, our faith will be replaced with the reality of heaven.

"In this you greatly rejoice, though now for a little while, if need be, you have been grieved by various trials, " **Vs. 6 NKJV**

Just the mere thought of our promised reward for our faith and to be able to share in that reward with God for eternity brings to us great joy. This joy is so great that the temporary trials and sufferings that we must endure on this earth is of little concern to us. Trials and sufferings are not something that we desire to have come upon us but if the do, or should I say, when they do the glory of reward will supersede them all.

Jesus told us that we were to "expect" trouble, but with the inevitability of trouble our mind is comforted by the presence of Jesus and we can be of good cheer; for in our present trouble we find Jesus with us. **John 16:33** Trials are with us but we can be genuinely glad, we can have authentic joy and can live with the happy thought that God is with us, He is for us and He will never leave us and is for certain, come back for us.

"that the genuineness of your faith, being much more precious than gold that perishes, though it be tested by fire, may be found to praise and honor, and glory at the revelation of Jesus Christ," **NKJV Vs. 7**

Genuineness means authenticity, the real thing and nothing about it is artificial. Genuineness comes from prove; it comes from knowing that it will stand the scrutiny of the most severe test because it is the real thing. Peter tells the reader that as the purity and genuineness of gold is made better by fire, so is the testing of our faith made better and becomes pure and therefore more valuable to us by the testing. When gold is tested and all the impurities that have attached itself have been burned away there is nothing but pure gold left. In the same mannor the believer becomes more and more pure by our testing and the impurities melt away all that is left is gold and that gold brings joy to the owner.

God allows the testing and with the testing we come to see Him more clearly, we give Him greater praise, honor. The completion of our testing will become gloriously evident at the "revelation" of Jesus Christ. We will be like Him!

"Whom having not seen you love. Though now you do not see Him, yet believing, you rejoice with joy inexpressible and full of glory." **NKJV Vs. 8**

Here again our faith is defined: *"having not seen you love."* Our love for Jesus is expressed by our faith: *"yet believing"* Peter says you rejoice anyway because our faith some how causes us to see the invisible One. We cannot explain it, we cannot understand it fully ourselves but we feel it, we know it and it brings to us an inexpressible joy in our realization of it and we are full of glory. Our cup is beyond full to the point of running over with joy. Have you ever been so happy and so full of joy because of something that has just happened? At that moment when asks you how you feel, nothing comes out? You find yourself at a lost for words because there are no words that can fully describe your feeling. This is what Peter is writing about. The glorious thought of God and what He has done for us has left us with our jaw dropped and at a lost for words in "inexpressible" or "unspeakable" joy. Though we do not deserve this gift, it is graciously and mercifully given to us. Unbelievable!

"receiving the end of your faith-the salvation of your souls." **NKJV Vs. 9**

Having received our salvation, our faith has completed its work in us and now we have realized the promised gift is no longer a promise, it is received. We have our hands on it and our eyes are beholding the gift. The gift is the fulfillment of the promise of God, we are with Him and in His Kingdom.

Of this salvation, the prophets have inquired and searched carefully, who prophesied of the grace that would come to you, searching what, or what manner of time, the Spirit of Christ who was in them was indicating when He testified beforehand the sufferings of Christ and the glories that would follow. To them it was revealed that, not to themselves, but to us they were ministering the things which now have been reported to you through those who have preached the gospel to you by the Holy Spirit sent from heaven-things which angels desired to look into." **NKJV Vs. 10 - 12**

This gift is *"the salvation of your souls."* This salvation is what the prophets wrote about but did not completely understand; they just obeyed and wrote what the Holy Spirit led them to write. After they wrote it they tried to figure out when this was going to take place. They prayed about it, they studied it, they searched other scriptures that had been written but with all their prayer, study and searching they came up with no clear understanding of how this would take place, when this would take place and why it would take place. They believed what they wrote but did not understand it completely. How could God suffer? How could the

Messiah come in the form of man? Why would God save those who were not of the nation of Israel?

The believer today finds himself in the same situation as we read of the return of Jesus and all that is involved in the last time and in those days. We do not understand when it will take place; we don't completely understand how it will take place other than it will take place at the command of God. We believe it but most of us disagree as to the *"manner of time"*.

The answer is that we do not need to understand completely but we do need to believe and obey the Word of God. As the Old Testament writers wrote without a clear understand, we are to believe without a clear understanding. What we do understand is that God is good, He cannot lie and He is in total control of all things. Nothing can happen but what He does not completely understand. Did you know that nothing can happen to you but has not first been filtered through the fingers of God and with His approval? Though we do not understand, God does, so our responsibility is to trust Him Who knows us best and desires for us only what is best for us and for His glory. That is what the prophets understood.

Not only the prophets seek understanding but the angels in heaven eagerly watched with great anticipation how it all worked out. It is with this same believing spirit that we are to trust God and do what He has given us to do. What God has given us is the Good News of His great kindness and love. Paul spoke of it as he left the believers in Ephesus. In **Acts 20:24** he tells them that life is not worth living unless we spend it doing the work that God has given us and that work is to tell others of His great kindness and love that leads to the gift of eternal life in Christ Jesus. We don't have to understand the how, we only need to obey completely in faith.

"Therefore, gird up the loins of your mind, be sober, and rest your hope fully upon the grace that is to be brought to you at the revelation of Jesus Christ; as obedient children, not conforming yourselves to the former lusts, as in your ignorance; but as He who called you is holy, you also be holy in all your conduct. Because it is written, 'Be holy, for I am holy." **NKJV Vs. 13 - 16**

So, Peter writes, because of this faith and in the grace of a good and glorious God who knows all and works all things for us, rest. Rest in the understanding that we do have; and remembering how God has displayed Himself to be faithful thus far in our lives; forget everything but God and our understanding of Him so far and think with a clear mind not a cluttered and doubting mind; move forward trusting God and eagerly anticipating our receiving our promised reward in heaven.

Our problem is to be distracted in our everyday life by what is happening around us and then our progress slows down or comes to an unexpected halt. Peter warns the reader to not take their eyes off Christ; he encourages them not to be conformed to the world but Christ Jesus. That is also what Paul wrote in **Romans 12:2**; he tells us not to be "conform" to the world but to be "transformed" by the renewing of our minds. The believer needs to be constantly renewing their minds in order to be transformed into that godly mind that God desires for us to have. A renewed mind is an undistracted mind; it is a new mind, a strengthened mind and a mind that is confident in the "Renewing" of our mind.

A mind that has been renewed by God is a set apart mind, and sanctified and holy mind because it is like the mind of Christ. Holiness is the desire of God and it is not something to be shunned or ashamed. If we are to commune with a holy God we must have the mind of the holy God. As Jesus did not consider it a reproach to come before His Father, we too must not consider approaching the throne of God robbery or taking away something from God. Our fellowship is what God desires; our fellowship is why He sent His Son in the first place. Did you know that the hearts desire of a holy God is to have fellowship with you? He does desire our fellowship and has written in Scripture that we should be holy because He is holy. **Leviticus 11:44**

"And if you call on the Father, who without partiality judges according to each one's work, conduct yourselves throughout the time of your stay here in fear; knowing that you were not redeemed with corruptible things, like silver or gold from your aimless conduct received by tradition from your fathers, but with the precious blood of Christ, as the lamb without blemish and without spot" **NKJV Vs. 17 – 19**

God judges rightly and He shows no favoritism. He is righteous and just in all His ways.
"It is a fearful thing to fall into the hands of the living God." **Hebrews 10:31 NKJV** *"The Lord is righteous in all His ways, Gracious in all His works."* **Psalm 145:17 NKJV**

Yes, God is righteous and He is holy; so how can a holy God cause the believer to come with confidence before His throne? We can come boldly before His throne because he is loving, gracious and merciful. What brings about this confidence is because of our response to His invitation of forgiveness. We can come with confidence because we are His children and the sheep of His pasture. We can come boldly because we have the righteousness of His Son Jesus upon us and we are, in His eyes, as pure and holy as His Son. This was done because Jesus was made to be our sin and we were given in return His righteousness. **2 Corinthians 5:21** God is not <u>partial</u> but He is <u>perceptive</u>. When the believer comes before Him with the righteousness of His Son upon them, the Father sees His Son and His righteousness not ours that is filthy. **Isaiah 64:6**

"He indeed was foreordained before the foundation of the world, but was manifest in these times for you who through Him believe in God, who raised Him from the dead and gave Him glory, so that your faith and hope are in God." **NKJV Vs. 20 & 21**

"Foreordained" means pre-determined or decided upon at an earlier time. Foreordained means that an act was already concluded before it began. Here Peter tells us that before the very foundational things of creation was set into action God already had a plan for redemption.

There is no way that any created being can have a clue of an understanding about being "foreordained"; that is an ability of the Creator and not His created creature. What foreordained does do is that it brings about a confidence in us that God has everything under control and we can trust Him. Foreordained confirms the plan of God and it is why that plan is realized by us and caries with it a comfort in knowing we are as secure as God's Word is true. God knows what He is doing and we don't have to know what He knows. We just need to know Him.

When Jesus came to this earth with the promise of peace on earth and good will to men; the conclusion of His mission was as sure as the promise of God. All of this brought, what the angel proclaimed in **Luke 2:14** great glory to God in the highest and on earth peace good will toward men.

"Since you have purified your souls in obeying the truth through the Spirit in sincere love of the brethren, love one another fervently with a pure heart." **NKJV Vs. 22**

Now we are striving to be holy as God is holy and our confidence is in Him and we have the understanding He is in control and He loves us just because He wants to love us. We know that this love is unmerited by us then we must have that same type of love within us toward the rest of our fellow believers. We don't need to be looking at what others are not doing but thankful for what they are doing. We need to pray for our fellow believers in Christ Jesus and encourage them as they live their lives for Christ. We need to be looking out for their well being and to be thankful for them.

The problem is that we notice error way before we recognize success and assets. We have a great proficiency in judging and a deficit in loving and commending. We are not the judge or jury we are the servant. We need to have fervent love for our fellow believers and we also need to have a pure heart and mind as we work with them.

"having been born again, not of corruptible seed but incorruptible, through the word of God which lives and abides forever, because all flesh is as grass, and all the

glory of man as the flower of grass. The grass withers and it's flower falls away, But the word of the lord endures forever. Now this is the word which by the gospel was preached to you." **NKJV Vs. 23 – 25**

"not of corruptible seed but incorruptible," What is that seed that is in us? In **Genesis 1:11** we read: *"Then God said, 'Let the earth bring forth grass, the herb that yields seed, and the fruit tree that yields fruit according to its kind, whose seed is in itself, on the earth.' And it was so."* **NKJV**

The seed is the life-bearing product of the tree, plant or creature. The seed will produce another of its own kind. This is the plan we see of the Creator in **Genesis**. Every fruit bearing thing had within it the element that brought for another of its own kind.

Jesus tells the parable of the wheat and the tares or weeds and in that parable, He relates what corruptible seed is. Corruptible seed is a foreign seed not like the original planted seed. The corruptible seed was spread by an enemy, an evil one. For the believer, our enemy is The Evil one and that is the Devil or Satan.

"So, the servants of the owner came and said to him, 'Sir, did you not sow good seed in your field? How then does it have tares? . . . He answered and said to them: He who sows the good seed is the Son of Man. The field is the world, and the good seeds are the sons of the kingdom, but the tares are the sons of the wicked one." **NKJV Matthew 13:27; 37 & 38**

John writes that the good seed is the seed of God and the seed of God produces the fruit of the Spirit: Love, joy, peace, longsuffering, kindness, goodness, faithfulness, gentleness, and self-control. **Galatians 5:22 & 23**

The seed of the flesh is the works of the flesh and they produce fleshly works: adultery, fornication, uncleanness, lewdness, idolatry, sorcery, hatred, contentions, jealousies, outburst of wrath, selfish ambitions, dissentions, heresies, envy, murders, drunkenness, revelries, and the like. **Galatians 5:19 – 21**

John writes: *"Whoever has been born of God does not sin for the seed remains in him; and he cannot sin, because he has been born of God."* **NKJV 1 John 3:9** When the believer starts seeing evil things in his life he must realize that the evil one has been spreading bad seed. He must ask himself the question: How did this happen? If we want to find out what happened then we must submit to God and He will show us what is wrong in our lives; and then he must make an assertive effort deal with the problem and to resist the devil and he will run; and then draw near to God and he will find that God will draw near to him. **James 4:7 & 8**

God's good seed is incorruptible and it will not fade or pass away, the good seed of God it will endure forever. The seed of God doesn't get stale, lose its power or fail in anyway; it endures forever. The seed of God gives us eternal life because that what it produces. We can depend upon this and if God said it then there is no need to doubt it; it is His sovereign promise.

Chapter Two:

"Therefore, laying aside all malice, all deceit, hypocrisy, envy, and all evil speaking, as new born babes, desire the pure milk of the word, that you may grow thereby, if indeed you have tasted that the Lord is gracious." **2:1 – 3 NKJV**

With this understanding here, how is the believer to live his life. There is much to lay aside or put down in the quest for building and living a spiritual life in Christ Jesus. All the characteristics of this world that are native to it must be done away with, each build upon the other. Look at these:

1. **Malice**: The desire to cause harm to another. It carries with it an angry spirit.

2. **Deceit**: Not being truthful but being crafty, self-serving and cunning.

3. **Hypocrisy**: Not real but a life that is a lie and lived in the dark.

4. **Envy**: Not satisfied with what you have but always wanting what someone else has and it causes hate to build in your life.

5. **Evil speaking**: Verbalizing the hate and ill will that is in your heart. It **creates** malice in the heart

of others that you desire to make a disciple and team mate.

Each of these characteristics contradict the Christian character that we have. None of these characteristics reflect Christ nor do they give glory to God. All of these are tools of Satan; each supports the other to build a life opposite that of a godly life.

We are new creations of God and babies in this new life in Christ. Therefore, we need to desire what it takes to grow in this new life in Christ. A baby begins its growth by consuming milk only, so we as new born babes in Christ must feed on the milk of the Word of God. We will later move into fruits and vegetables and then comes the meats. As our body in Christ grows so will our desire for more solid food, as our body become able to digest them.

There is a caution here, Peter brings up the obvious and this is: *"if indeed you have tasted that the Lord is gracious."* To grow as a Christian believer, one must be a Christian believer. There is no such thing as an almost Christian; you either are a Christian or you are not a Christian. It is possible for people to be around believers and benefit from their lives but not actually be a believer or real follower of Christ. These types of individuals enjoy the fellowship of believers but never seem to be able to understand, or should I say, never able to transform to a new life. They cannot because they have not actually tasted that the Lord is gracious. These individuals live lives of confusion because they can't grow and they can't grow because they have not been born again as a New Creation.

If you find yourself to have a life of confusion then ask God to make you a New Creation; ask Him to work within you that new life. What is happening is that you still have *malice, all deceit, hypocrisy, envy, and all evil speaking* in your life. If you do not have the power of God in your life, you cannot lay aside the works of the flesh in your life. You need New Life in Christ. You need to repent of your sins and take the free gift of salvation that Jesus died for you to have.

"Coming to Him as to a living stone, rejected indeed by men, but chosen by God as precious, you also, as living stones, are being built up a spiritual house, a holy priesthood, to offer up spiritual sacrifices acceptable to God through Jesus Christ.
"Therefore, it is also contained in the Scripture, Behold, I lay in Zion a chief cornerstone, elect, precious, and he who believes on Him will by no means be put to shame." **NKJV 2:4 - 6**

As we grow in Christ we begin to build a life in Christ as well. God gives to each of His children a mission, a job or purpose in life as His followers. What the believer does is carry the Good News of Christ Jesus and develop disciples: *" Go, therefore and make disciples of all nations, baptizing them in the name of the Father and of the Son and of the Holy Spirit, teaching them to observe all things that I have commanded you and lo, I am with you always, even to the end of the age."* **NKJV Matthew 28:19 & 20**

"Teaching them to observe" is making a disciple of them; it carries with it the aim to teach them what we know, and having taught them what we know reminding them of what they have learned until what they have

learned has become part of them, and they continue to grow daily.

The word *"living stone"* means that Jesus was the foundation stone, and though rejected by the world, was chosen by the Father, totally acceptable to the Father for the building of this new house, this new building and this new creation. He was precious to the Father. We too are precious, chosen and commissioned to build our house for the Lord and to help others in building a house in the Lord.

We are priest or we can go to God personally, we can ask forgiveness of our sin, we can ask for guidance personally and boldly; we can do all this with confidence that He hears us, He desires us and we have been made totally acceptable to the Father because of the righteousness of His Son Jesus. **2 Corinthians 5:21**

" Therefore, to you who believe, He is precious; but to them who are disobedient, the stone which the builders rejected has become the chief cornerstone and a stone of stumbling and a rock of offense. They stumble, being disobedient to the word, to which they also were appointed," **NKJV 2:7 & 8**

The same Stone that is a blessing to some is an offense and cause for stumbling through life to others. The Stone is a sure fortress to the believer but a crushing Stone to the non-believer or disobedient. The Stone has become their judgment and condemnation to eternal death but to the believer that same Stone brings comfort, security, protection and promised eternal life. This Stone is an appointed Stone, a prophesied Stone. To one the Stone brings blessing and reward while to the other it brings cursing and judgment.

"But you are a chosen generation, a royal priesthood, a holy nation, His special people, that you may proclaim the praises of Him who called you out of darkness into His marvelous light." **NKJV 2:9 & 10**

Not only are we blessed by God but we are a *"chosen generation"*. God's chosen people is the Nation of Israel. God told Abraham that he would make his name great and that he would be the father of a people through which He would use to display to the world how he works. **Genesis 12:1 – 3**

Peter points out that the believer and follower of Christ is a "Chosen generation". We have been chosen to bring to this earth the Good News of how God has chosen to redeem this people in this sinful world and that is the work of His Son Jesus.

Not only are we a "Chosen generation" but a "royal priesthood". The priesthood was that group of people who had been selected to lead the people in worship and teach them the Scripture. The believer is a representative of the Great High Priest Jesus Christ.

We are a "chosen generation" we are a "royal priesthood" and we are also "a special people". The believer has been selected as the chosen generation to carry the Good News and has been blessed in having a royal responsibility to teach Scripture and lead in worship to God as representatives of God and because of this we are special people. There has never been a generation or a priesthood throughout history who has had anything near the great honor of what we have been given. We have a special blessing and a special purpose unlike non other in all time. We have the personal honor of being called to share our eye witness account of how we have been called out of darkness into a marvelous light. *"For it is the God who commanded light to shine out of darkness, who has shone in or hearts to give the light of the knowledge of the glory of God in the face of Jesus Christ. But we have this treasure in earthen vessels, that the excellence of the power may be of God and not of us.."* **NKJV 2 Corinthians 4:6 & 7**

We are to demonstrate God's goodness to those whom we find ourselves around.

"who once were not a people but are now the people of God, who had not obtained mercy but now have obtained mercy." **NKJV 2:10**

Why would God select us? Certainly not because of any good we may have done, after all, our best of our good is nothing but filthy rags in the eyes of God. **Isaiah 64:6**

The reason for God selecting the believer is because of God's mercy. Mercy is not giving to someone what they deserve. I am so thankful that God is merciful. If God gave us what we deserved He would be exercising His justice. Yet, God, though He is just is also merciful, and He displays mercy to whom ever He wishes. *"For He says to Moses, 'I will have mercy on whomever I will have mercy, and I will have compassion on whomever I will have compassion."* **NKJV Romans 9:15**

So God selects us because He desires to do so in the light of his all knowingness or omniscience; what a blessed though that is and what a wonderful truth that is. This mercy comes by our faith in Him and the forgiveness by Him.

"Beloved, I beg you as sojourners and pilgrims, abstain from fleshly lusts which war against the soul, having your conduct honorable among the Gentiles, that when they speak against you as evildoers, they may, by your good works which they observe, glorify God in the day of visitation." **NKJV 2:11 & 12**

Peter begs or beseeches the believers here, desires, implores, deeply encourages them to give great care, to give much thought toward or to take aggressive steps toward being a holy follower of Christ Jesus. Paul uses the same emphatic use of the word in **Romans 12:1**. *"I beseech you therefore brethren. . . "*

Following Christ Jesus is not an easy thing that just comes naturally, it comes spiritually. There is a great battle in the life of a Christian, it is a battle of the flesh against the spirit as Paul describes:

Galatians 5:16 & 17 *"I say then: Walk in the Spirit, and you shall not fulfill the lust of the flesh. For the flesh lusts against the Spirit and the Spirit against the flesh; and these are contrary to one another, so that you do not do the things that you wish."* **NKJV**

Ephesians 6:10 – 12 *"Finally, my brethren, be strong in the Lord and in the power of His might. Put on the whole armor of God, that you may be able to stand against the wiles of the devil. For we do not wrestle against flesh and* *blood, but against principalities, against powers, against the rulers of darkness of this age, against spiritual hosts of wickedness in the heavenly places. Therefore, take up the whole armor of God, that you may be able to withstand in the evil day, and having done all, to stand."* **NKJV**

Romans 8:5 *"For those who live according to the flesh set their minds on the things of the flesh, but those who live according to the Spirit, the things of the Spirit."* **NKJV**

Peter wants the believer to understand that the Christian life is exactly what Jesus had said: *"In this world you will have trib*ulation.*"* **John 16:23 NKJV** Therefore, he begs them to live their lives cautiously and pro-actively engaged by abstaining from fleshly lusts. This is a war that we are engaged in and it involves the leader of the rebellion who is non-other than the warriors of evil and Satan himself. He is a roaring lion who seek someone to devoir. **1 Peter 5:8**

The believer is a sojourner and pilgrim in that we are not citizens of this earth. Our citizenship is in God's Kingdom and we are traveling through this earthly, fleshly place carrying the Good News to it's citizens. The effect of the Good News is that the person who joins us gains citizenship to the Kingdom of God as well. Those individuals become Children of God also.

"fleshly lust" They are warring against us in our bodies are personal and natural desires that are human desires and not godly desires. We have a human nature because we are human but the believer has another life that has been born again within him and that life is a spiritual life. We will not fully be freed from the human nature until

we put off this old body to receive our new body made for the new heaven and the new earth.

The goal of the believer in this battle is to develop a conduct in life that is "*honorable*" and noticeably honorable to all around us in that it goes against the natural. It is so noticeable that as the non-believer begins to slander us for the good that we are doing and calling that good evil because our good works contradict everything that they intended to do.

Now, we must remember that we may have to die for what we believe on this earth but we must remember as well, to be absent from the body is to be present with the Lord. **2 Corinthians 5:8,** and we read in **Philippians 1:21** *"For to me, to live is Christ, and to die is gain."* **NKJV**

Having a clear understanding of events, demands that we see the event from beginning to end. Therefore, as a sojourner and a pilgrim on this earth we must know where we end our journey. We do not end our journey here on earth, we end or conclude our journey with Christ. Jesus told the thief on the cross that the cross was not the end, it was just the beginning for on that day he would be with Jesus in paradise. **Luke 23:43**

When Jesus intervenes for us and comes back to judge the world, the conduct of the believer will be remembered by God and for the things that we did well we will be given a reward and He will receive the glory for our godly conduct as sojourners and pilgrims on this earth. This earth is not our goal, our goal is Jesus and to be with Him in His home and on our "new earth".

"Therefore, submit yourselves to every ordinance of man for the Lord's sake, whether to the king as supreme, or to the governors, as to those who are sent by him for the punishment of evildoers and for the praise of those who do good. For this is the will of God, that by doing good you may put to silence the ignorance of foolish men- as free, yet not using liberty as a cloak for vice, but as bondservants of God. Honor all people. Love the brother hood. Fear God. Honor the king." **2:13 – 17 NKJV**

Good conduct involves not only our manor of life but our relationship to those around us. The success of the believer is judged by how others see the believer. They see how the believer lives, what he does and how he talks. They see where he goes. How the believer lives speak volumes to those around him about what is important to him.

The believer is not to plot, scheme and develop plans to overcome the opposition to the mission that God has given him. The believer is to obey, go and do what he has been commissioned and empowered to by. We are commissioned by Jesus and we are empowered by the Holy Spirit and are to go in His might not our own. Peter says: *"For this is the will of God, that by doing good you may put to silence the ignorance of foolish men- as free, yet not using liberty as a cloak for vice, but as bondservants of God."* It is true that the believer is free and has great liberty and where the Spirit of the Lord is there is liberty (**2 Corinthians 3:17 NKJV** *"Now the Lord is the Sprit; and where the Spirit of the Lord is there is liberty."*) but the believer is <u>never</u> to use that freedom that he has to the harm of others by allowing his action to cause anyone to sin. (**Galatians 5:13 NKJV** *"For you, brethren, have been* *called to liberty; only do not use liberty as an opportunity for the flesh, but through love serve one another.")*

Good conduct caries with it the mandate of how the believer relates to others and how others view him. Nonbelievers do not live for God because that is not their nature, though we may disagree greatly with what they do and despise the sin that characterizes their lives we do not need to see them as our enemy. They are not our enemy, they are the recipients of the Good News; they are the focus of our mission that we have been given and have been commissioned to carry. We are delivering mail to them and the letter is the Good News from Jesus Christ.

It is difficult to honor bad kings but there is no adjective that has been given to the noun, king. At the time, Peter wrote his epistle or letter, Nero was the Emperor of Rome. We might not like the ruler of our country or the ordinances and laws that they make but we are asked to submit to them *"for the Lord's sake".* We are "commanded" to "submit" to the king. That is not easy but it is Gods will. **(vs. 15)** Peter also expressed this as Peter, James and John we taken before the high priest in **Acts 5:28 & 29** that when it came to a command that was directly against the command of God, a believer ought to obey God rather than man. That was the exception to ordinances and laws.

The believer ought to pray about everything that he does and make sure that he is living honorably before God and man.

The believer is commanded to honor leaders: national leaders; state leaders, county leaders; city leaders and community leaders. *"Therefore I exhort first of all that supplications, prayers, intercessions, and giving of thanks be made for all men, for kings and all who are in authority, that we may lead a quiet and peaceable life in all godliness and reverence. For this is good and acceptable in the sight of God our Savior. Who desires all men to be saved and to come to the knowledge of the truth."* **1 Timothy 2:1 – 4 NKJV**

Paul writes that God has appointed the king. *"Let every soul be subject to the governing authorities. For there is no authority except from God, and the authorities that exist are appointed by God. Therefore, whoever resists the authority resist the ordinance of God, and those who resists will bring judgment on themselves. For rulers are not a terror to good works, but to evil. Do you want to be unafraid of the authority? Do what is good, and you will have praise for the same."* **NKJV Romans 13:1 – 3**

The king has been sent by The King of kings for the purpose of punishment to evildoers. Peter points out that kings are also used by God to observe and praise believers for good works and that those good works were done in obedience of God and for the praise and glory of God. This does not mean that nothing bad will happen; but that we should be judged by others for doing good in the sight of God, for the cause of God and let God take care of the kings and rulers that He has sent. God judges, God shows mercy and God blesses. So blessed be the name of The Lord! Rest in God and in the power of His Word.

Good works will contradict and silence the ignorance of sinful mankind. Now the believer should never try to out smart or out maneuver the workings of mankind for the battle is the Lords after all. Never use good works, Peter points out, as a cloak, and undercover maneuver evil under the guise of helping God out.

The believer has liberty in his life but there is never an occasion for him to use that liberty to do what he desires to do. The believer is to obey God and to do the will of God. The believer is not to decide what God's will is for him, he is to discover God's will and having discovered it, not to question God's known will at any time.

In short, Peter concludes, honor everyone. Love your fellow believers; fear God above all and give honor to the king. This is the will of God.

"Servants, be submissive to your masters with all fear, not only to the good and gentle, but also to the harsh." **2:18 NKJV**

Servant, slave, laborer each of these words apply to a person who is under the control of, indebted to, or employed by another person; a person who works for another.   The word slave will give a clearer understanding of what Peter means by being in submission to as a master. Peter tells the reader to be submissive not because someone is kind, gentle or understanding but even if they may be unkind, rough and have no desire to have any consideration for there well-being. We are to give proper respect for improper treatment. Why? Because of Jesus.

The words good, gentle or harsh mean that in spite of how we are treated, our treatment has no bearing as to why we should be submissive, the reason is because it is commendable and because we are more concerned about pleasing God rather than man. We treat them gracious because God has been gracious to us. Grace is unmerited favor and it is extended out of our desire to be like Christ not because of any benefit we have received and therefore want to the return the favor.

"For this is commendable, if because of conscience toward God one endures grief, suffering wrongfully. For what credit is it if, when you are beaten for your faults, you take it patiently? But when you do good and suffer, if you take it patiently, this is commendable before God. For to this you were called, because Christ also suffered for us, leaving us an example, that you should follow His steps: 'Who committed no sin, Nor was deceit found in His mouth.' Who when He was reviled, did not revile in return; when He suffered, He did not threaten, but committed Himself to Him who judges righteously; who Himself bore our sins in his own body on the tree, that we, having died to sins, might live for righteousness-by whose stripes you were healed." **NKJV 2:19 - 24**

The believer's responsibility on this earth is to carry the Good News or The Gospel of Christ to a lost and dying world. We are offering to them the forgiveness of sin that all need; we are presenting to them purpose in life and eternal life to all who would believe the Message. This is our job, we are bond-slaves of Christ Jesus, we are labors together for the cause of Christ. We are commissioned to carry the Gospel to all not because that they are good, kind and gentle but in total disregard of how they might treat us. Our "Godly conscience" gives us the challenge to endure harsh treatment and grief in this world.

It is of no value, Peter, reminds the reader, to endure trouble if we deserve trouble. The value is enduring trouble in exchange for our doing good. Remember Jesus tells us that we are to expect harsh treatment and trouble in this world. **John 16:33**

Jesus is our patter for service and living a godly life and we should strive to follow that example and walk in His steps. Jesus suffered for deeds of good, He never threatened people for their evil actions to Him. Jesus, healed sick people, fed the hungry, delivered from impending danger, He taught people, He encouraged the discouraged, warned the wandering and offered forgiveness for the sins of all who would believe. Yet, in spite of all His goodness he was hated, cursed, evil spoken of, plotted against, beaten, tortured and crucified on a cruel cross. Why? Because of the grace and mercy that He offered all who would believe. He was unjustly treated. Pilate, after a trial of Jesus gave the official verdict: *"I find no fault in this man."* **NKJV Luke 23:4** *"I am innocent of the blood of this just person."* **NKJV Matthew 27:24** Still the people ask for Him to be unjustly punished. Jesus is our example and we should follow Him in His steps.

Jesus, never expressed any deceitful word for being abused and unjustly treated. Because Jesus set the example, therefore, we to should do the same with others. The beating that Jesus endured, the stripes that He bore brought to us the gift of righteousness for the healing of our sins against God and now we are free from the penalty of sin, which is eternal death. Now we have eternal life.

For you were like sheep going astray, but have now returned to the Shepherd and Overseer of your souls." **NKJV 2:25**

We once were going down the wrong road that led to eternal death but now things have changed. Repentance, is a turning around, it is a change of direction and that is what happens to the believer at the point of repentance; we turn around. No longer are we headed down the path to eternal death in hell but to eternal life in God's heaven.

Did you know that hell was not created for mankind but for Satan and his angels? All of mankind who have refused God's gift of eternal life will receive their reward of everlasting fire in hell, as an intruder. *"Then He will also say to those on the left hand, 'Depart from Me, you cursed, into the everlasting fire prepared for the devil and his angels. "* **NKJV Matthew 25:41**

Heaven and hell is a choice we must make. Which will you take? Jesus died for you; will you live for Him? Submit to Him.

Chapter 3

"Wives, likewise, be submissive to your own husbands, that even if some do not obey the word, they, without a word, may be won by the conduct of their wives, when they observe your chaste conduct accompanied by fear." **NKJV 3:1 & 2**

God is good and He never does anything or requires anything that would not be for our good and His glory, ever. God is the very essence of love and good. There is none good but One, Jesus reminds the Rich Young Ruler in **Matthew 19:17.**

God was not belittling the Christian believer- citizen by asking them to be submissive to rulers and kings and was not suggesting that a slave was less of a person by being submissive to the master. Peter was giving examples as to how a believer can glorify God in their relationship with others. Everything that we do ought to be for the reason of giving glory to God and not ourselves.

Remember the question that was directed to Jesus by the Pharisees in **Matthew 22:36 – 40**? They asked the question. Which is the great commandment in the law? The response of Jesus was two-fold: *"You shall love the Lord your God with all your heart, with all your soul and with all your mind. This is the first and great commandment and the second is like it: 'You shall love* *your neighbor as yourself.' On these two commandments hang all the Law and the Prophets.' "* **NKJV**

Notice how we are to love the Lord our God:
- With all our heart
- With all our soul
- With all our mind

Our love for God must take our giving to Him our whole being. We are to give everything in displaying our love to Him. In the same manner we are to give our whole being displaying God's love to others with our whole self. Jesus is our example in this. We are to walk in His steps.

Now with this in mind, the same love must be displayed in our home life. Peter says *"likewise"* with the same fervor and ambition in life of being submissive to God be submissive to your husband. Not because he is better, he is not; but because God ask of us to do so. The reason is to display a godly conduct, a Christ like spirit.

Many women in the early church were married before they became a believer and their husbands were not believers. This made life very difficult for them. The best thing to happen, of course, would be for the husband to become a believer. But that was not the situation in, at least, some if not most homes. Therefore, the women were to be living examples before their husbands through their conduct in the home and in their daily life; the husband then would see Christ in them and the wife would allow the Holy Spirit to work in his life. The Holy Spirit is the one Who draws people to Christ. Having been convicted, the husband and then become a believer and grow in his new life. God would be using the women as a daily Bible for their husbands to read.

The word *"fear"* does not mean to be in dread of, worried of danger or of an expectation of suffering punishment or harm in some way but fear here means to have a reverent loving respect or honor for the responsibility that God has given to their husband. This is not saying women are not as important as men or wives are of less value than the husbands, it is not. The idea here is only position of responsibility. Peter is dealing with relationship here in a God glorifying way. God is a God of order and all that He does has order, purpose and direction. We can see an order of relationship from God the Father to the Son of God to the Holy Sprit, to the angels, mankind and all the way down through His church, believers and family. There must always be a leader and the leader must be know to all to be the leader and the leader must be faithful in carrying our his responsibility of being a leader.

"Do not let your adornment be merely outward-arranging the hair, wearing gold, or putting on fine apparel-rather let it be the hidden person of the heart, with the incorruptible beauty of a gentle and quiet spirit, which is very precious in the sight of God." **NKJV 3:3 & 4**

Adornment means how a one dresses and how one presents themselves to others. Peter is not writing here suggesting that a lady should not be concerned about dressing herself up and not to try to look good or "presentable" to others. Everyone should have that concern about their outward appearance. What Peter is saying is that a lady should not be "only concerned" with the outward putting on of apparel to be "adored" but to have great concern about how we look from the inward person. It is the inward person, *"the hidden person of the heart,"* that makes up the real person and it is that hidden person that people adore. The inward person is the "incorruptible" beauty, that quiet spirit of a person that draws the attention of God and which He is concerned about. The inward person is precious in the sight of God. Do others "adore" you for what you are on the inside?

"as Sarah obeyed Abraham, calling him lord, whose daughters you are if you do good and are not afraid with any terror." **NKJV 3:6**

A daughter learns from their mother. A daughter keeps her house as her mother taught he by caring for their home. A daughter cooks, cleans, dresses, and talks in a similar manner as her mother. Peter is suggesting that these early believers have for their example the matriarch Sarah, the wife of Abraham set a example for them to follow. Sarah was beautiful, she was loved by Abraham; cared for by Abraham and she was adored by Abraham and it was with that knowledge of Abraham that she had no fear of Abraham. Sarah knew that Abraham loved her and she could always count on him.

The phrase *"calling him lord,"* means that she accepted her place of responsibility in the home as in the care of Abraham. She understood that God who was Abraham's Lord and was her Lord as well had given Abraham a responsibility of leadership; and therefore, she was in agreement with that. It does not suggest that there was any worship to be given here to Abraham by Sarah his wife. The whole purpose of this whole passage from **2:11 – 3:12** is relationship and attitude toward others. This passage is all about loving God and loving others.

"Husbands, likewise, dwell with them with understanding, giving honor to the wife, as to the weaker

vessel, and as being heirs together of the grace of life, that your prayers may not be hindered." **NKJV 3:7**

Solomon in **Proverbs 4:7** writes: *"Wisdom is the principal thing; therefore, get wisdom, and in all your getting, get understanding."* Having a good understanding of a situation makes for a happy person. You can have great wisdom but if you do not know how to use that wisdom, you lack wisdom. Being able to quote the Bible is one thing but an correct understanding of what you read and how to obey it is the major objective of the believer.

Peter exhorts husbands to have a good understanding of their responsibility under God in the building of the home. If the husband messes up, the home is messed up. The home hinges on passion to please God and the trustfulness of the husband. The husband "must" give honor to the wife, and if he does, the wife will have no problem with her God given position as a wife in the home. If the wife does not give honor to the husband, she is disobeying God.

"As to the weaker vessel" means that women, in general, do not have the physical strength of a man and therefore the husband must physically care for her and must maintain the understanding that the grace of God has been equally given to each. All sinful humanity needs the grace of God; there is no exception. So, everyone is equal and everyone needs God's grace not only for salvation but in the work God has given them. We must also have a clear understanding that we are all equal in the sight of God.

The phrase *"that your prayers may not be hindered."* Means if the husband is disobedient to the Word of God and disobedient in his position and responsibility God has given him in the home, his prayers will be hindered because he is out of the will of God. It means that the husband must repent of his sin and make his life right with God. If the husband is not in tune with his wife, he is not in tune with God. If you are not in tune with God the conversation with God is hindered or it is awkward.

"Finally, all of you be of one mind, having compassion for one another; love the brothers, be tenderhearted, be courteous; not returning evil for evil or reviling for reviling, but on the contrary blessing, knowing that you were called to this, that you may inherit a blessing. For He who would love life and see good days, let him refrain his tongue from evil, and his lips from speaking deceit. Let him turn away from evil and do good; let him seek peace and pursue it. For the eyes of the Lord are on the righteous, and His ears are open to the prayers; but the face of the Lord is against those who do evil." **NKJV 3:8 – 12**

Now let me bring this all together, Peter says, the mind-set of the believer is to be of one mind. The goal is to dwell in unity of the Spirit. If we are in the Spirit we have the fruit of the Spirit flowing through us and we see others as God intends us to see others.

Compassion is prominent, love is evident, a tender heart is relevant in our daily lives and no one is trying to get the advantage over another. We seem to live in a "me first" society. Everyone is out to get the prominence over another. They say we live in a "dog-eat-dog-world" and it seems to be true. But for the believer there must be an obvious difference. We should not return evil for evil we should give blessings to others because we have been blessed and we will soon inherit blessings greater still.

If we love life and we desire to have a good relationship with others then we should see others as God sees them. We need to pursue life with a happy heart, and gain control of the way we talk about others. Speak good things and look for good things to do for others. God is all knowing and all seeing; God sees all things and hears all things. God has a loving ear to His children and an arm of vengeance upon those who dishonor Him.

"And who is he who will harm you if you become followers of what is good? **NKJV 3:13**

The natural response to a good deed is a good reception. When good is done, good is generally returned and life is more pleasant.

"But even if you should suffer for righteousness' sake, you are blessed. 'And do not be afraid of their threats, nor be troubled.' But sanctify the Lord God in your hearts, and always be ready to give a defense to everyone who asks you a reason for the hope that is in you, with meekness and fear; having a good conscience, that when they defame you as evil doers, those who revile your good conduct in Christ may be ashamed. For it is better, if it is the will of God, to suffer for doing good than for doing evil." **NKJV 3:14 - 17**

Suffering is part of the believer's life. We need to remember this. Jesus suffered and warned that we too would suffer because we are not to think that we are better than the Master **John 13:16;** in this world, we are to expect trouble. But don't fear trouble, do not be afraid of threats of punishment. God is always with us and the Holy Spirit is supplying us with all that we need to do all that God has called us to do.

Suffer if we must but always set aside the Lord our God in our heart. We can take comfort in Him. We don't need to plan what to say to others but we need to know what to say to others if they ask us why we do what we do. We need to be able to explain to others why we have the hope that is within us. People will notice that the believer is different and they will enquire of us what the reason is.

One problem that everyone must deal with in the midst of suffering and attack is not to respond in kind but to have meekness about us. Now meekness is not weakness, meekness is power under control. Remember we have within us the power of God but vengeance is not ours it is Gods. Vengeance comes when God decides to give it and in the way in which He desire to deliver it. The believer is the bearer of The Good News not bad news.

When the believer does bear undeserved punishment at the hand of the nonbeliever, it will bring about to him a realization of his unjust actions and therefore our unjust suffering will stand as a ever present proclamation of conviction to the evildoer. Remember, if it is God's will for you to suffer, then it is a blessing to you for you are engaged in doing God's good will. When the believer suffers, God will with the evil intentions and evil deeds of others, bring about His good intention.

"For Christ also suffered once for sins, the just for the unjust, that He might bring us to God, being put to death in the flesh but made alive by the Spirit, by whom also He

went and preached to the spirits in prison. Who formerly were disobedient, when once the Divine longsuffering waited in the days of Noah, while the ark was being prepared, in which a few, that is , eight souls were saved through water." **NKJV 3:18 – 20**

Jesus suffered for us! If He suffered, should we be discouraged or feel disappointed because we suffer? Never look at those believers around you who seem not to be suffering in your eyes. Don't look at others, look at Christ Jesus, He suffered for your sins. Jesus suffered unjust punishment for it was our punishment, yet, He did not open His mouth, He did not complain because His suffering was why He came. **Isaiah 53:3 – 9** Why should any believer feel he is above suffering? Isn't that an arrogant thought?

Jesus died and He suffered but it was the final sacrifice for sin. **Hebrews 10:12 NKJV** *"But his man, after He had offered one sacrifice for sins forever, sat down at the right hand of God."* After His sacrifice and death He arose from the grave to conquer, sin, death and the grave for the believer. He did it all for us. We had no part in that suffering or sacrifice. Therefore, why would we complain for having to suffer in the carrying of the Good News to others?

For some reason this portion of Scripture presents a problem to many believers: *"but whom also He went and preached to the spirits in prison. Who formerly were disobedient, when once the Divine longsuffering waited in the days of Noah, while the ark Then the Lord saw that the wickedness of man was great in the earth, and that every intent of the thoughts of his heart was only evil continually." as being prepared, in which a few, that is, eight souls were saved through water."* I think the reason for the difficulty is that perhaps many do not want to believe this.

"He went and preached to the spirits in prison." Who are these people? They are those who had died in the judgment of God in the days of Noah. Why did they die? Everyone else were rebels and despisers of God and their lives were totally evil " and Why did they die? Because they rejected the warning of God to repent of their sins. (*Then the Lord saw that the wickedness of man was great in the earth, and that every intent of the thoughts of his heart was only evil continually."* **Genesis 6:5 NKJV**

The whole population of the earth, with the exception of Noah's family, rejected God and God judged them through water and they died physically, but because of their rejection of God they would also eternally die spiritually again by fire.   In **Genesis 6:3** we have recorded the mind of God: *"And the Lord said, 'My Spirit shall not strive with man forever, for he is flesh yet his days shall be one hundred and twenty years.* **NKJV**" and in **vs. 6 & 7** *"And the Lord was sorry that He had made man on the earth and He was grieved in His heart. So the Lord said I will destroy man whom I have created from the face of the earth, both man and beast, creeping things and birds of the air, for I am sorry that I have made them."*

These people had been held in captivity awaiting a verdict and now the verdict was in and it was read to them.   This is the message of Jesus to these captive people who are doomed to eternal fire. Jesus preached this to them. How you may wish to interpret it beyond what is written is your choice. I choose to take it at what I see written. The truth is that what God does is what God has done and I am not the judge of His decision to give mercy, grace or anything else He may decide to do.

Romans 9:15 & 16 NKJV *"For He says to Moses, 'I will have mercy on whomever I will have mercy, and I will have compassion on whomever I will have compassion. So then it is not of him who wills, nor of him who runs, but of God who shows mercy."*

The Messiah had been promised in **Genesis 3:15** *"And I will put enmity between you (Satan) and the woman, and between your seed and her Seed; (Jesus) He (Jesus) shall bruise your head, and you shall bruise His heel."* **NKJV**) They rejected God.

Noah and his wife along with his three sons and their wives were saved because they entered into the Ark that God had prepared for them. There were only eight people in the whole population of the world that were followers of God; everyone else were, disobeyers, rebels and despisers of God and their lives were lived in and with completely evil thoughts and deeds. These people had announced to them the final judgment of God and the Only Begotten Son of God proclaimed that judgment to them, Jesus Christ.

"There is also an antitype which now saves us-baptism (not the removal of the filth of the flesh, but the answer of a good conscience toward God). Through the resurrection of Jesus Christ, who has gone into heaven and is at the right hand of God, angels and authorities and powers having been made subject to Him." **Vs. 3:21 & 22 NKJV**

An "antitype" is a picture and it is talking about the ark as being a picture of salvation for us. It is an example, perhaps that we can use to understand this work of God. The resurrection of Jesus was the sign of the competed work of God for our salvation or for our redemption from the penalty of sin being death. Jesus conquered sin and the grave. **1 Corinthians 15:56 & 57 NKJV** *"The sting of death is sin, and the strength of sin is the law. But thanks be to God, who gives us the victory through our Lord Jesus Christ."*

Jesus is the only way and the only sacrifice that can save us. Thanks, be to God for His wonderful gift. **Acts 4:12 NKJV** *"Nor is there salvation in any other, for there is no other name under heaven given among men by which we must be saved."*

"Therefore, God also has highly exalted Him and given Him the name which is above every name, that at the name of Jesus every knee should bow, of those in heaven, and of those on earth, and of those under the earth, and that every tongue should confess that Jesus Christ is Lord, to the glory of God the Father." **Philippians 2:9 – 11 NKJV**

As surely as the believer is saved by the work of Jesus, this same Jesus is going to return again, just as He said. He now is in heaven preparing a place for His followers; **John 14:1 – 4 NKJV** *"Let not your heart be troubled, you believe in God, believe also in Me. In My Fathers house are many mansions, if it were not so, I would have told you. I go to prepare a place for you, and if I go and prepare a place for you, I will come again and receive you to Myself, that where I am there you may be also. And where I go you know and the way you know."*

When the time arrives for Him to come again, He will come. As Jesus ascended into heaven the angel reminded His followers: **Acts 1:11** *". . . men of Galilee, why do you stand gazing up into heaven? This same Jesus, who was taken up from you into heaven, will so come in like manner as you saw Him go into heaven."* **NKJV**

Chapter 4

"Therefore, since Christ suffered for us in the flesh, arm yourselves also with the same mind, for he who has suffered in the flesh has ceased from sin, that he no longer should live the rest of his time in the flesh for the lusts of men, but for the will of God." **Vs. 1 & 2**

Now, suffering is a part of the believer's life as we have established; expect suffering; endure suffering with a mind of understanding and use it in your daily life to help develop a life not associated with sin.

Have you ever noticed that suffering causes the believer to turn to God; it turns his eye to God for help because He is our only help. If our eyes are on Christ it is not fixed on sinful things. *"for he who suffered in the flesh has ceased from sin."*

The believer's goal is to be more and more like Christ and to be holy as He is holy. We don't want to live our lives for the glory of men or in the ways of men but for the glory of God and in the ways of God because this is, after all, the will of God that we live that way.

The way of God is not like the ways of man, they are the opposite of each other. The way of God contradicts the ways of the world. The way of God is foolishness to the eyes of the world. The mindset of the world is completely opposite of God mind and His sure view of everything. The believer is never to use the thinking of the world to shape his thinking; if he does he will be led astray. Therefore, he must look to God's Word for direction, instruction and reformation. Where does the believer finds truth in guidance? He finds it in the Word of God and through His Holy Spirit only.

Hebrews 4:12 NKJV *"For the word of God is living and powerful, and sharper than any two-edged sword, piercing even to the division of soul and spirit, and of joints and marrow, and is a discerner of the thoughts and intents of the heart. And there is no creature hidden from His sight, but all things are naked and open to the eyes of Him to whom we must give account."*

"Yes, and all who desire to live godly lives in Christ Jesus will suffer persecution." **2 Timothy 3:12 NKJV** The believer is a "peculiar person" and odd person to the world but a special person to God. *"who gave Himself for us, that He might redeem us from every lawless deed and purify for Himself His own special people, zealous for good works."* **NKJV Titus 4:14**

"For we have spent enough of our past lifetime in doing the will of the Gentiles-when we walked in lewdness, lusts, drunkenness, revelries, drinking parties, and abominable idolatries. In regard to these, they think it strange that you do not run with them in the same flood of dissipation, speaking evil of you. They will give an account to Him who is ready to judge the living and the dead," **Vs. 3 – 4**

Luke tells of Paul's farewell to the church at Ephesus in Acts **20:24** that life is not worth much unless we use it to do the work that God has given us to do. Doing the will of God is the goal of the believer. Here in **1 Peter** we have a similar exhortation. Peter says to the reader that they have spent enough of there lives living like the majority of the world (*doing the will of the Gentiles.*).

What is that way?
- Lewdness: Immoral and shameful things.
- Lusts: Self-fulfilling desires of all types with no concern for others.
- Drunkenness: Not having self-control but controlled by something else.
- Revelries: Rioting, carousing, and looking for things to do that cause destruction.
- Drinking parties: Finding people of like desires to join you in your evil mindless actions.
- Abominable idolatries: Totally against God, to seek out others to not only live with but to worship with in an anti God life style. Having no regard to God's holiness.

That is the life style of the world and the world cannot understand why you would not want to join with them in there lifestyle. You may have been one of them before you were saved and they cannot understand why you no longer have there desires and they talk about you. They make fun of you in their own worldly way; they want to demean you, to slander you and to try their best to tear you down. They want you back.

But the truth is, they will have to give an account of each evil deed that they do against you on that awful day of judgment in which God Himself will judge the living (those who were alive at the time of His coming.); and the dead (those who have died). No one escapes the judgment of the Lord.

"For this reason the gospel was preached also to those who are dead, that they might be judged according to men in the flesh, but live according to God in the spirit." **Vs. 6**

The Gospel was preached and many died at the hand of men for preaching the Gospel, but that was not the end for the believer in Christ Jesus. The earthly life of the believer is spent proclaiming the Good News and after the earthly death of the believer comes eternal life in Christ Jesus. The believer will live forever just as God has promised that they would. This earth is only a temporary thing, our eternal home is in God's Kingdom. The home for the believer, is that new heaven, the new earth that New Jerusalem that will be coming down out of heaven upon the new earth. **Revelation 21:1 & 2** *"Now I saw a new heaven and a new earth, for the first heaven and the first earth had passed away. Also, there was no more sea. Then I, John, saw the holy city, New Jerusalem, coming down out of heaven from God, prepared as a bride adorned for her husband."* **NKJV**

"But the end of all things is at hand, therefore be serious and watchful in your prayers. And above all things have fervent love for one another, for love will cover a multitude of sins. Be hospitable to one another without grumbling. As each one has received a gift, minister it to one another, as good stewards of the manifold grace of God." **Vs. 7 –10**

Things may seem bad now, but this is not the end; it will come and it will come sooner or later, but it will come. For sure it is nearer now that when we first believed. **Romans 13:11 – 14 NKJV** *"And knowing that the time, that now it is high time, to awake out of sleep; for now our salvation is nearer than when we first believed. The night is far spent, the day is at hand, Therefore, let us cast off the works of darkness, and let us put on the armor of light. Let us walk properly, as in the day, not in revelry and drunkenness, not in lewdness and lust, not in strife and envy. But put on the Lord Jesus Christ, and make no provision for the flesh, to fulfill its lusts."*

Time, I remind you, means nothing to God (because He is eternal **2 Peter 3:8 NKJV** *". . . do not forget this one thing, that with the Lord one day is as a thousand years, and a thousand years as one day."*)

Today is not a time to be slack in our passion or in our prayers, now is the time to be serious about what we believe. Now is the time to be observant of what is happening around us. Now is the time to be praying for everyone and everything.

The main thing for us is not to get angry about what is happening but diligent in our spreading the Good News because of what is happening. We can best express this fervency by our love for each other. We need to address all of our disagreements with the fuel of love because love will easily cover all those disagreements that we might have. We don't need to be more concerned about how we are treated but how we treat others. *"Love covers a multitude of sins."*

What does that love look like? It takes the shape of hospitality to one another. Ask yourself: "Am I being hospitable to people?" How can you be hospitable to someone? What do you need to do? Now as you are exercising hospitability, don't be grumbling about the lack of hospitability of someone else.

What has God given you to do? What is the gift that is yours? Use that gift that you have received and display the grace of God. Not because of something someone has done for you but because they don't deserve it. Grace is "unmerited favor".

"If anyone speaks, let him speak as the oracles of God. If any ministers, let him do it as with the ability which God supplies, that in all things God may be glorified through Jesus Christ, to whom belong the glory and the dominion forever and ever. Amen." **Vs. 11**

What are the oracles of God? An oracle is a message that has been given to give to another. If God has given you a message make sure that you are speaking what God has given you, not what you feel someone needs to hear. You could be wrong but God is never wrong. God is truth. If you are going to speak, put yourself totally out of the message. Present God's Word as it is; proclaim God's Word as it is and allow God to speak through you *"as he supplies"* making sure He receives all the glory. We have no claim to any glory at all, all the glory belongs to God and to Him alone. He is the rightful receiver of all glory at all times and in all seasons. His glory is forever! Amen!

"but rejoice to the extent that you partake of Christ's sufferings, that when His glory is revealed, you may also be glad with exceeding joy." **Vs. 13**

Our glory is in Christ. Our glory is in the suffering for Christ. When Christ comes again we will be glad that He gave us the opportunity to suffer for Him and we will have great joy in that knowledge. I like those words: *"with exceeding joy."* To exceed is to go beyond what you start with. In **Ephesians 3:20** Paul tells us that God is able to do and to "exceed" any expectation we may have. He goes way beyond our wildest dream of what He might do. His exceeding work gives us exceeding joy. Suffering is trumped by the great and exceeding joy that we have in Christ Jesus.

"If you are reproached for the name of Christ, blessed are you, for the Spirit of glory and of God rests upon you. On their part He is blasphemed, but on your part He is glorified." **Vs. 14**

Don't be overcome with the grief of suffering, be overcome with the joy of suffering for Christ Jesus. Though those who bring the suffering think they are challenging God through their profanity, they are in actuality increasing their crime against God and the severity of their judgment. They will pay for their actions but you will be bringing glory to God.

"But let none of you suffer as a murderer, a thief, an evildoer, or as a busybody in other people's matters." **Vs. 15**

Make sure that your suffering is because of Christ, not because of evil actions as those who bring a reproach to God. If your suffering is because of murder, stealing, evil actions or intentions and because of seeking ways to talk about someone else to bring shame or slander them; you are bring shame to Christ and you deserve to suffer for your evil doings just as the unbeliever does. You may not be a murderer, thief or criminal but if you are a "busybody" then you are just as bad. Jesus came to redeem the world not add to their crimes and sins. The believer ought to be a follower of Christ Jesus and walk "in His steps". **2:21**

"Yet, if anyone suffers as a Christian, let him not be ashamed, but let him glorify God in this matter." **Vs. 16**

To be ashamed is to be sorry for your actions. Never be sorry for what you do for Christ Jesus. It is an honor to serve and suffer for Him. Suffering is a badge of honor not a punishment for what you have done. Suffering brings glory to God. Have you noticed how often suffering is mentioned? Never try to get out of suffering, use suffering for the glory of God. It shouts to the world: "I am a follower of Christ Jesus!"

"For the time has come for judgment to begin at the house of God; and if it begins with us first, what will be the end of those who do not obey the gospel of God?" **vs. 17**

Think about this: if God will surely judge a child of His, how much greater will be the judgment of those whom He does not know as His child!

"It is a fearful thing to fall into the hands of a living God." **Hebrews 10:31 NKJV**

"Therefore, we must give the more earnest heed to the things we have heard, lest we fall away. For if the word spoken through angels proofed steadfast, and every transgression and disobedience received a just reward, how shall we escape if we neglect so great a salvation, which at the first began to be spoken by the Lord and was confirmed to us by those who heard Him." **Hebrews 2:1 – 3 NKJV**

"Now if the righteous on is scarcely saved, where will the ungodly and sinner appear? Therefore, let those who suffer according to the will of God commit their souls to Him in doing good, as to a faithful Creator." **Vs. 18 & 19**

Bottom line: Commit all that we do to Christ Jesus; commit the good things, the great things, the everyday things and commit those times of suffering to Christ as well. Consider all things as a gift from the good hand of God. Commit them all as a goal to reach and blessing and something worthy of praise.

Remember God is faithful in all things and He is faithful at all times. God make even the bad time, useful in fashioning great things.

Chapter 5

"The elders who are among you I exhort, I who am a fellow elder and a witness of the sufferings of Christ, and also a partaker of the glory that will be revealed:" **vs 1**

Peter begins to close his letter here in Chapter five by expressing his joy and appreciation to the leaders of the church. He exhorts them, he desires to encourage them to be strong and steadfast in any coming persecution or suffering that they may be placed under. He tells them that he is a fellow leader or elder as well. He is also a personal eye witness of the sufferings of Christ. Peter saw Jesus suffer, Peter suffered, he witnessed the suffering of others and has witnessed the conclusion of suffering. The conclusion of suffering always brought glory to God. Suffering did not quiet the Good News, it enflamed the Good News. Suffering did not cause others to quit but gave them greater ambition and strength.

The greatest glory will not be realized on this earth but in God's Kingdom at the feet of Jesus where every knee will bow and acknowledge Him as God's Son. **Philippians 2:9 – 11** *"... that every tongue should confess that Jesus Christ is Lord, to the glory of God the Father."* **NKJV**

"Shepherd the flock of God which is among you serving as overseers, not by compulsion but willingly, not for dishonest gain but eagerly, now as being lords over those

entrusted to you, but being examples to the flock;" **vs. 2 & 3 NKJV**

These words are to those elders, leaders or pastors of the church. Peter commands them to serve as an overseer or servant. The pastor is not boss, he is an overseer or the person who has been given the responsibility of watching the flock unto the Shepherd returns.

The pastor should not see his responsibility as an obligation that he has to do, but as something he desires to do to prove himself to be a faithful servant. The pastor should not see his mission as a way to make money by hook or crook, but he ought to be eager and anxious to do his best, as a mission of entrustment and carry out that mission by being an example to the flock and prepare them to make disciples who would be able to make disciples as well. Paul but it this way as he taught Timothy: *"And the things that you have heard from me among many witnesses, commit these to faithful men who will be able to teach others."* **2 Timothy 2:2 NKJV**

"And when the Chief Shepherd appears, you will receive the crown of glory that does not fade away." **Vs. 4**

Through the ministry of shepherding a body of believers many times is a difficult one and perhaps even a thankless one; it is Jesus who is the Chief Shepherd who will reward His servant. The reward that we may receive here on this earth, will not endure but the reward that God gives His servants will last for eternity. This specific reward for the under-shepherd is a crown of glory that will not fade away. Rewards are not always enduring ones.

One additional note is that believers will be able to lay those rewards at the feet of Jesus. Can you imagine the feeling of honor that is associated by personally laying at the feet of Jesus a valuable medal of valor?

When soldiers receive medals of valor and service, it is a proud moment and the suffering that that medal represented is quickly forgotten for the glory that he receives. The President of the United States awards the Medal of Honor to a soldier; he is the one that drapes it around the neck of the recipient and it is rewarded for uncommon acts of bravery that goes above and beyond the call of duty. There is honor there but it pales to the honor of laying a crown at the feet of Jesus, Who alone is worthy of such honor and glory.

"Likewise you younger people, submit yourselves to your elders. Yes, all of you be submissive to one another, and be clothed with humility, for God resists the proud, but gives grace to the humble. Therefore, humble yourselves under the mighty hand of God, that He may exalt you in due time, casting all your cares upon Him, for He cares for you." **Vs. 5 - 7**

In the same manner younger people should display humility to those who are older than they are. Learn from their successes and learn from their failures. Every one should make it your aim to put down the natural bent to pride, and desiring the high places. Work hard in the road of life and learn to recognize the haughty people and stay away from them. Haughty people want to take advantage of you and they will hurt you. God gives undeserved favor to the humble but He turns from the haughty. Put your hand in the hand of God and when you do you will find great joy.

Never look at the things that cause grief in your life, fix your eyes upon God who genuinely cares for you. God is always with us and He will never leave us or forsake us. We need to be like God challenged Joshua. **Joshua 1:5 & 6**

"Be sober, be vigilant, because your adversary the devil walks about like a roaring lion, seeking whom he may devour. Resist him, steadfast in faith, knowing that the same sufferings are experienced by your brotherhood in the world." **Vs. 8 & 9**

Our fight is not against flesh and blood but against principalities, powers and workers of iniquity in heavenly places: Paul tells us in **Ephesians 6:12.** It's not people that we are fighting it is Satan and his buddies. Satan is our adversary and he is crafty, he works by stealth. He makes devilish plans for our destruction. He can't battle God for He is all-powerful. Satan can, however, hurt us and cause us great harm if we stand alone.

The way to battle Satan is to resist him but that is not easy. We need to have the armor of God in place in our battle **Ephesians 6:13 – 18**. We need to be suited up, prayed up and keep our eyes lifted up to the source of our strength, our God and Savior. We should never let our guard down because it is when you think that you have it under control that the great attack comes. He who thinks he stands, take heed lest he fall, we read in **1 Corinthians 10:12.** The believer is encouraged because he is not the only one in the battle; because believers all around the world today and through out all history have been in this great battle. But resist the devil and he will flee. That is a promise.

"But may the God of all grace, who called us to His eternal glory by Christ Jesus after you have suffered a while, perfect, establish, strengthen, and settle you." **Vs. 10**

The God of all grace, the God of all unmerited favor, the God Who shows no favoritism but does show His favor; may the God who has called us just because He is loving, gracious and kind; may this God of grace who is preparing a special home for His children not because of what they have done but because of Who He is and what He has promised; may this Jesus that Peter is writing about and that he has seen; may this same Jesus Whose name is above all others and who is worthy to be praised above all; may He give you grace.

He gives us grace to endure, He gives us grace to understand that what we are suffering will only be for a while, for a limited time but in that time we will be perfected, we will be made better; we will be set on a firm foundation, on a sure foundation in Christ Jesus. We will be confident in the faith within the family of God forever.

"To Him be the glory and the dominion forever and ever. Amen." **Vs. 11**

The final chapter concludes in eternity and throughout eternity Jesus will be the only recipient of great honor and glory. Upon this statement, there can be no shadow of turning. To be able to be part of such glory is marvelous beyond description.

"By Silvanus, our faithful brother as I consider him, I have written to you briefly, exhorting and testifying that this is the true grace of God in which you stand." **Vs. 12**

Silvanus (**1 Thessalonians 1:1** *"Paul, Silvanus, and Timothy,)* is Silas, the same Silas that was with Paul after Paul's split with Barnabas. **Acts 15:37 – 41** Why Silas was with Peter here at this moment is not clearly known but he was and he was also there with Timothy, Paul's protégé and son in the Lord. (**1 Timothy 2:2**)

The endearment that Peter expresses to Silas, Timothy and Paul displays the great respect and admiration that all the apostle had for each other. Peter refers to him as *"our faithful brother".* Peter confirms to the readers that his aim in writing is to encourage and to give a reliable witness to the Gospel of Christ Jesus because they knew he was one of the closest group of the disciple of Jesus. He was truly an eyewitness and lived with Jesus during His ministry, suffering, death, resurrection and ascension back into heaven.

"She who is in Babylon, elect together with you greets you; and so does Mark my son." **Vs. 13**
She who is in Babylon may refer to Rome but Peter is talking about the believers or the church, *"elect together".* The church where Peter is desires to say hello or sends their greeting to the scattered church.

Mark, the nephew of Barnabas (**Acts 15:39**) the same Mark that Paul writes about in as has shown himself to be useful in the ministry. **2 Timothy 4:11** What this displays to us is that even though a believer has made a wrong choice in the early part of their Christian life, they still can prove to be a valuable asset to the cause of Christ. Never look at times of failure but learn from failure and look for opportunities to serve Christ Jesus all through out life.

"Greet one another with a kiss of love. Peace to you all who are in Christ Jesus. Amen." **Vs. 14**

The kiss of love is a greeting that not only the believers but all people of the day would greet one another. In many European and Middle Eastern countries still today greet each other in this manor. Love is the icon of the early church, they were know by their love. *"By this all will know that you are my disciples, if you have love for one another."* **John 13:35**

The final exhortation is peace. Not just any peace but the peace of God; the peace that Jesus was talking about to His disciples. *"Peace I leave with you, My peace I give to you, not as the world gives do I give to you. Let not your heart be troubled, neither let it be afraid."* **John 14:27 NKJV**

It is this peace the dispels all fear and leave peace. The worlds peace fades, the worlds peace cannot be counted upon but God's peace will never leave you and your heart will never be troubled or fearful again in His peace. It is this *"Peace"* that Peter desires for them. Notice that the Peace is capitalized. It is capitalized because it is God's Peace.

Amen! As it is written so shall it be!

Just the Basics

Discovering the Truth in an Untruthful World

Commentary on Second Peter
By
Danny Glenn Thomas

Introduction

"The task of the scholar is to guarantee the purity of the text; to get as close as possible to the word as originally given. He may compare Scripture with Scripture until he discovers the true meaning of the text, but right there his authority ends. He must never sit in judgment upon what is written. He must not bring the meaning of the word before the bar of his reason." **A. W. Tozar**

This second letter [**2 Peter 3:1**] from the Apostle Peter [is to the scattered or dispersed church (*Diaspora*). Scattered because of persecution. [**1 Peter 1:1 NKJV** *"Peter, an apostle of Jesus Christ, to the pilgrims of the Dispersion . .*] have been taught and to expose or make them aware of false prophets and teachers that would come with ever increasing regularity. [**2:1**]

Gnostics had begun to infiltrate the early church and this cunning and dangerous heresy came by stealth to carry away the new and unsettled believers. Gnosticism would become a great danger to the early church and it still has it's hand upon many believers as well as churches today.

A Gnostic believes in knowledge is the supreme thing in understanding God. It is a dualistic or dualism view of God. The Gnostic does not believe that a divine being could ever be mixed with a creation of matter. Gnosticism was well established in Greek culture before it was mixed into Christianity. Knowledge was the primary thing not based on faith. The Gnostic have the understanding that there is an inferior god who created matter and is written about in the Old Testament and a superior God whom Jesus, as Redeemer revealed to man. They believe that created matter is foreign to God because matter is evil and God is a God of Knowledge and He will not and cannot be part of evil matter; this is the dualistic character of God. They believe that Jesus as God's Son was transcended upon earth and not incarnate or born of a virgin. In other words Jesus came down to earth but was not born upon the earth.

This Knowledge is a secret knowledge that is given to certain people but not to all. Those who have been chosen can understand and relay that knowledge to others. The Gnostic believes that the chosen knowledge receivers can do anything that they want because they have been exempt from the punishment from the sin of this world. The Gnostic is a superior creation and those who are not the chosen are in subjection to them.

Therefore this is the context under which Peter writes his letter to remind the believers of what true Christianity is and what they have learned already and to help them remember. [12 – 15]

The church today is still damaged by this Gnostic Gospel. The world tries to inject into the thinking of the church today of other Gospels, false doctrines, as equal to and even superior to the Good News of Jesus. The "Dead Sea Scrolls" contain many of those Gnostic writings and confuse many believer and seekers as well.

Chapter 1

"Simon Peter, a bondservant and apostle of Jesus Christ." **Vs. 1**

Peter begins the letter by identifying himself as a bondservant. A bondservant is a slave that has been freed by his master. Although, having been given freedom from his master and can freely make decisions freely, he purposefully and willfully chooses to remain under the care of his one-time master. He willingly wants to remain with his master out of his love for him and his master's great love for him. **Deuteronomy 15:16 – 17 NKJV** *"And if it happens that her says to you, 'I will not go away from you', because he loves you and your house, since he prospers with you, then you shall take an awl and thrust it through his ear to the door, and he shall be servant forever. Also to your female servant you shall do likewise."*

Peter told Jesus: *"If I have to die with you, I will not deny you!"* **Mark 14:31 NKJV** This reveals Peters intention, although he did deny Jesus. Peter wanted to be with Jesus and desired to serve Him even if it meant death. He did fail then but soon he would indeed die for his Master.

Peter calls himself, and was, a bondservant of his Master. The question to us is, is it our desire to be found faithful in our mission on this earth even if it means death? We must remember that, upon this earth, death is lest than a moment, it comes in less than the twinkling of the eye. For the believer, death is a door, for to be absent from the body is to be present with the Lord. Our mission here upon earth is to do the will, or the work that has been given us by our Master Jesus Christ. Like Peter, we too have freely chosen to be His bondservant. We are here to do His will not our own will. **Philippians 1:21 NKJV** *"For me to live is Christ, and to die is gain."* *"For we are confident, yes, well pleased rather to be absent from the body and to be present with the Lord."* **2 Corinthians 5:8 NKJV**

The apostle Paul wrote in **Acts 20:24 NKJV** *"But none of these things move me; nor do I count my life dear to myself, so that I may finish my race with joy, and the ministry which I received from the Lord Jesus, to testify to the gospel of the grace of God."* For the believer, to live is to do that which we have been given to do. Life on earth is not to do our will but God's will.

For the Gnostic, life here on earth is to do what was pleasing and profitable for himself, the Gospel commands just the opposite; life it to do what is pleasing and profitable to God. The work of the bondservant is the work of the master.

Peter chooses to be a bondservant but he was chosen to be an Apostle. He was selected by the Lord Jesus Christ to be a disciple. Peter, lived with Jesus for more than three years and He personally witnessed all that Jesus did and said.

The requirement for being an Apostle was to personally be taught by Jesus and therefore see Him visibly. The twelve disciples were Apostles and Paul was one as well. Paul refers to himself as an apostle born out of due time or I could say, out of sequence. **1 Corinthians 15:8 NKJV** *"The last of all He was seen by me also, as by one born out of due time."* Peter gives credibility to Paul as he refers to the writings of Paul as a beloved brother: **2 Peter 3:15 NKJV** *"and consider that the longsuffering of our Lord is salvation-as also our beloved brother Paul, according to the wisdom given to him has written to you."* Paul defends himself as a true apostle: *"Am I not an apostle? Am I not free? Have I not seen Jesus Christ our Lord? Are you not my work in the Lord?* **1 Corinthians 9:1 NKJV**

"To those who have obtained like precious faith with us by the righteousness of our God and Savior Jesus Christ:" **Vs. 1b**

Peter identifies those to whom he is writing this epistle or letter. Peter writes to those believers who have come to a faith in Jesus Christ in the same way and in the same manor as he had. That faith, that trust, that hope in anchored solely in and upon Jesus Christ. The quality of faith is totally upon Jesus and it is completely dependant upon the work, the payment of Jesus for the sin of the believer; it is the righteousness of Jesus upon the believer that completes us, plus nothing. I cannot emphasize this enough, that work of redemption was achieved totally by Jesus and the only thing that the believer must do is to accept that work alone. He does this by asking forgiveness for his sin, and asking is to believe that Jesus is the only begotten Son of God. As Paul writes in **Ephesians 2:8 and 9 NKJV** *"For by grace you have been saved through faith, and that not of yourselves it is the gift of God, not of works, lest anyone should boast."* And in **2 Corinthians 5:21 NKJV** *"For He made Him who* *knew no sin to be sin for us, that we might become the righteousness of God in Him."* In **Ephesians 2:19 NKJV** *"Now, therefore, you are no longer strangers and foreigners, but fellow citizens with the saints and members of the household of God."*

This is the *precious faith* that Peter is speaking. Our faith is in Christ alone and by faith alone. We are no less a citizen of heaven than Peter and the Apostles are because of the perfect work of Jesus. Remember when we begin to add anything to the work of Jesus we lessen the quality of Jesus; we are saying that His sacrifice and His blood was not enough. It was more than enough. In **Hebrews 10:12; 14** and **18** we read: *"But this man, after He had offered one sacrifice for sins forever, sat down at the right hand of God. . . For by one offering He has perfected forever those who are being sanctified. . . Now where there is remission of these, there is no longer an offering for sin."* **NKJV**

Jesus told Nicodemus in **John 3** that as sure as people were saved from death by looking at the serpent that Moses lifted up in the wilderness, Jesus Himself would be lifted up and that whoever would believe upon that work would be saved. *". . . that whoever believes in Him should not perish but have everlasting life."* **VS. 16 NKJV**

There is no work that can be added to the work of Jesus in order for a person to be forgiven and saved; there is no organization to become a member that is needed to fulfill the work of Jesus; there is no plus to be added after Jesus; there is no level of position that must be reached; Salvation is by Christ Jesus alone.

Works are not a condition that needs to be done for redemption but works are an expression of having received that redemption. We want to serve Christ, we want to be more like Christ, we want to do more for Christ because of what He has done for us. Behold how shall we escape if we neglect so great a salvation the writer of Hebrews tells us. **[Hebrews 2:3 NKJV]** **Romans 4:12** tells us that there is no other name given among men where by we must be saved. It is in Christ alone. Yes Jesus is the manifestation of the Grace of God that brings salvation and *"who gave Himself for us, that He might redeem us from every lawless deed ad purify for Himself His own special people zealous for good works."* **Titus 2:11 – 15 NKJV**

Jesus is our God and Jesus alone is our righteousness. When we are at our best, at our best time of life, doing our best work of all our life, that deed, that act of righteousness is but filthy rags in the sight of God the Father. **Isaiah 64:6 NKJV** *"But we are all like an unclean thing, and all our righteousness's are like filthy rag; we all fade as a leaf and our iniquities, like the wind have taken us away."*

It is a pleasant thought to know that it is because of what Jesus did for us that has secured for us an eternal home in His heaven. Jesus is good, Jesus is thorough and He knows all things past present and future. There is nothing that we might do, say or think but that He has always been aware and knowing all of that He offers to us redemption and eternal salvation. Yes, how precious a faith is that!

"Grace and peace be multiplied to you in the knowledge of God and of Jesus our Lord." **Vs. 2 NKJV**

Grace is unmerited favor; it is receiving something, which we totally do not deserve. It is an unbelievable gift, which cannot be explained other than it was given because the give desired to do so. Grace causes and brings about peace; it brings it about because it is undeserved. We don't deserve that grace so what could take it away? Can one do something that would be so undeserving of an undeserving gift? Grace is totally in the hand of the giver and the giver is God. The only reason for the grace is faith, trust in the credibility of the giver.

Now it is hard to understand how such a gift could be multiplied but Peter is saying that as the believer gains greater understanding of God's grace. When he begins to gain greater understanding of God and His character we become more and more confident and trusting of that grace gift. Knowledge brings to us more and more peace and a greater and greater understanding of God's great gift.

The believer should be a good student of the Word of God, Scripture. A student never stops studying, he never stops learning and he never comes to the point where he is satisfied with what he has learned. When we seek knowledge of God we begin to see greater things of His glory and we want to know more. The more we know about God the more we are able to help others and to share with others with what we have learned.

To multiply brings great results than to just add, multiplication of knowledge brings about larger answers than merely adding one small piece of data at a time. God promises to bring a greater increase in our knowledge of Him accompanied with greater and greater peace in life.

Vs. 3 *"as His divine power has given to us all things that pertain to life and godliness, through the knowledge of Him who called us by glory and virtue,"* **NKJV**

Another wonderful piece of knowledge is that as we live our life here on earth there will come many demands and challenges upon us both great and small. In all of these challenges of life we will come to find that we equipped for that challenge and begin to understand that we can do all things through Christ who is our strength and our supplier in life. **Philippians 4:13 & 19** This ever increasing knowledge gives us ever increasing peace.

But not only are we promised God's abundant hand in the things that pertain to our daily life but we are also promised His help, through the Holy Spirit, to teach and supply us power in our quest for godliness. The Holy Spirit is the Promised One that Jesus spoke of Who is our Counselor, Helper, Peace, Teacher and Empowerer. **John 14:16** *"and I will pray the Father, and He will give you another Helper, that He may abide with you forever-"* **NKJV**

This gift of knowledge also gives us greater understanding about how we can glorify God daily and helps us to develop within our daily lives virtue or moral excellence, as the **New Living Translation** renders it.

Vs. 4 *"by which have been given to us exceedingly great and precious promises, that through these you may be partakers of the divine nature, having escaped the corruption that is in the world through lust."* **NKJV**

What are these precious promises that are great and grow exceedingly?

- He promises us that He will be with us personally. **John 14:1 – 4**
- He promises us that He will forgive us of all our sins: past, present and future. **John 3:16**
- He promises us that He would come back for us. **John 14:2**
- He promises us peace. **John 14:27**
- He promises us the Holy Spirit. **John 16:13**
- He has promised us that we can be overcomers and more than conquerors through Christ Jesus our Lord. **Romans 8:37**

These are just a few of those precious promises that He has promised us. As we live our lives we come to discover that He is with us and He is able to help us do so much more than anything that we might ever ask, things way beyond anything that we could ever dream of asking. **Ephesians 3:20** This is a God thing that we have been called to do not a human thing and God things takes God ability. If He is with us it is He that is working through us and if God is for us, who is it that could be against us? **Romans 8:31**

These promises of Jesus have made us worthy of having direct access to Gods own nature in that we are like Him. Remember at creation that we were made in the image of God. **Genesis 1:27** It was sin that created a great gap between God and man and it was the sacrifice of Jesus closed that gap and opened the door where we might once again have that personal access to God. **Mark 15:38 NKJV** *"Then the veil of the temple was torn in two from top to bottom."*

"having escaped the corruption that is in the world through lust." We are part of this world but the forgiveness that we have received through Jesus, has made us exempt from the law of sin and death. **Romans 8:2** Can you understand that though we are in this world, we are not of this world? But being in this world, as strangers and sojourners through this world, we travel to our homeland, where our citizenship is recorded in the roll book of citizens of heaven. **John 8:23; Philippians 1:20** As we travel through this world, we are surrounded by and many times effected by, it's evil desires and corrupted values of earths citizens and leadership. But, we have our Kings great promise that there is an escape, there is a strong arm that is with us, and His supplied armor to have on to protect us and to give us an escape. When our escape is completed there is a great reward that we will be given.

Vs. 5 *"but also for this very reason, giving all diligence, add to your faith virtue, to virtue knowledge."* **NKJV**

Faith is the foundation of life in Christ. Christianity is not a "religion" it is a life in Christ, it is a faith. Faith comes from God and it is not a human attribute.

We live by faith. **Galatians 2:20** *"I have been crucified with Christ; it is no longer I who live, but Christ lives in me, and the life which I now live in the flesh I live by faith in the Son of God, who loved me and gave Himself for me."* **NKJV**

We work by faith. **James 2:26** *"For as the body apart from the spirit is dead, so also faith apart from works is dead."* **NKJV**

Now to this faith that we have in Christ Jesus, we begin to build our life in Christ and the first step is to add to our faith godly virtues or fruits of the Spirit. These fruits reflect the God that we serve. The process of addition takes great effort or diligence by the believer. This is not an easy task it is a never ending one that will require great attention all throughout our life.

If we understand where we are and having the knowledge of where we are going, we must understand that we must be very pro-active in our faith and with diligence, determine to become better each day we live; we must be ever adding to our faith, thus making that faith stronger. We strengthen our faith with virtue or a moral excellence that shines and stand out in our dark world.

Excellence is not bequeathed to someone; excellence is a goal; excellence comes with training, practice and being engaged. Excellence comes from endurance; excellence is something that one strives for. Excellence is achieved by the few not the many but it is recognized by all. Excellence shines through the dark; excellence is not normal it is abnormal. This is the virtuous life the believer is to strive toward. The believer strives for excellence because it is a reflection of The Excellent one, Christ Jesus our Lord.

Virtue is something that requires knowledge and learning. Knowledge is also something that takes time, effort and sacrifice. The believer must have a great desire to gain understanding of life to get through life. The Holy Spirit is our Teacher, Trainer, Helper and Counselor in our quest for knowledge. As we gain knowledge and as we become more and more proficient in our faith, we become stronger and our purpose and goal in life becomes more evident to us and understood. Things that once bothered us will no longer bother us for we have greater knowledge, greater purpose, virtue and faith.

Vs. 6 *"to knowledge self-control, to self-control perseverance, to perseverance godliness."* **NKJV**

No one wants to be out of control, we like to be in-control or self-controlled. God wants us to be self-controlled as well. God wants us to serve Him because we want to, because we choose to.

To become in control, a person must be able to see where he is, he must have the knowledge and the understanding that he is out of control before he can begin to gain self-control. *Self-control* is to be in manual mode and be able to clearly see his positioning; one must have an understanding of his environment, of the situation that he is in. Once he understands where he is and what must be achieved he can begin to make the proper adjustment to cause himself to be in control to get to where he wants to go.

Knowledge helps to bring about self-control and after you have gained self-control you begin to make purposeful plans to fulfill your goal. The goal of the believer is to be like Christ, to obey His commands and do the mission that He has personally given us. After we have that knowledge, plan and goal we start to make plans to do that work given us.

Perseverance is the next link and it requires patience. To persevere means to conquer or will over adversity and tribulation in life. Perseverance carries with it tribulation. *"And not only that, but we also glory in tribulation, knowing that tribulation produces perseverance; and perseverance, character, and character hope. Now hope does not disappoint, because the love of God has been poured out in our hearts by the Holy Spirit who was given to us."* **Romans 5:3 – 5 NKJV**

The result of perseverance is godliness and that godliness is a reflection of a God like character, fruit of the Spirit. *"But the fruit of the Spirit is love, joy, peace, longsuffering, kindness, goodness, faithfulness, gentleness, self-control. Against such there is no law."* **Galatians 5:22 & 23 NKJV**

Godliness relates us as being with God; it suggests that we are a-lined with God and can be numbered as one of His children. Godliness is a needed addition to the life of an over comer in life.

Vs. 7 *"to godliness brotherly kindness, and to brotherly kindness love."* **NKJV**

Brotherly kindness relates us to the family of God. As godliness makes our connection to God the next link in the chain is to the brotherhood, the family of God. Brotherly kindness is "love" for the brethren. Love is the icon of the believer. **John 13:35 NKJV** *"By this all will know that you are My disciples if you have love for one another."* *"These things I command you, that you love one another."* **John 15:17 NKJV** Brotherly love is a virtue or a moral excellence that the believer must have to be a strong and successful servant of God.

This chain that is being described by Peter for the believer is what will make for a successful, profitable and strong believer. Nothing happens without faith and our faith is from God. **Ephesians 2:8 NKJV** *"For by grace you have been saved through faith, and that not of yourselves; it is the gift of God,"*

Faith must be strengthened by the link of moral excellence, knowledge is next and it is followed by self control which brings about perseverance and the consistency of perseverance produces a godly life which is recognized by the world as we display the love of Christ and a Christ like spirit. This makes for a strong chain that will bring God glory and cause the world to see that we are genuinely Christian and true followers of Jesus Christ, the Only Begotten Son of God.

"For if these things are yours and abound you will be neither barren nor unfruitful in the knowledge of our Lord Jesus Christ." **Vs. 8**

These virtues in which we are striving must be ours, they must be part of us and having become a part of us they need to be in great supply in our lives. These virtues will be the fuel that brings to us a clear understanding of Christ Jesus and that clear understanding will create a confidently lived life, a successful ministry. We will be confident that we are in the will of God and that confidence is recognized by the joy our lives produce in us. We will be productive and we will be beneficial to the cause of Christ.

"For he who lacks these things is shortsighted, even to blindness, and has forgotten that he was cleansed from his old sins." **Vs. 9**

Shortsightedness is being near-sighted. A nearsighted person cannot see clearly from a distance, he stumbles around because he does not know the environment in which he is living. A shortsighted person is not much better that a blind person.

Why are these believers shortsighted? They are shortsighted because they have not been diligent in developing and caring for their Christian life. These believers have not been faithful in reading the Scriptures or praying to God and this inconsistency has caused them to forget what they, at one time, knew. Because they have developed this shortsightedness they live in uncertainty and fear has developed. There fear has come about by forgetting that they have been forgiven of their sin. If you think that your sins have not been forgiven then you are living a life of fear just as a non-believer. They are not fruitful, they are fearful.

"Therefore, brethren, be even more diligent to make your call and election sure, for if you do these things you will never stumble; for so an entrance will be supplied to you abundantly into the everlasting kingdom of our Lord and Savior Jesus Christ." **Vs. 10 & 11**

Peter has exhorted the believer to give diligence, to give special attention to improving their lives as a believer and not to give even greater passion in displaying to others that they are really true believers in Christ Jesus. How a believer is perceived as being genuine is very important. There should be no doubt to those around us that we are indisputability a believer in Christ Jesus.

The benefit of being diligent in proving that your calling is sure and indisputable is that the pull of the world, or the chance of you being misled into impure things that go against the life of a believer in Christ Jesus is lessened. This diligence increases the vision of the believer and stumbling in the Christian life won't be as much of a problem because his sight is more profound. In **Ephesians 5:15** the **New King James Version** uses the word *"See then that you walk <u>circumspectly</u>, not as fools but as wise."* So, the believer is encouraged in "<u>being careful</u>" how he lives, not careless as a fool would live but as the wise. The idea is to be looking all around you as you walk; to be looking intently for things that may cause you to stumble. It is foolish to go through our life on earth any other way. The **New Living Translation** uses these words in **vs. 16 of Ephesians** *"Make the most of every opportunity for doing good in these evil days."* The idea in **Ephesians** and here in **2 Peter 1:10** is living a Christian life on earth is not easy, it is difficult and caution must be used daily and at all times. A believer must live his life pro-active. The reward for our life in Christ is that our entrance through the gates of God's Kingdom will be a joyful one with an expectation of receiving great rewards and glorious crowns that we might lay at the feet of Jesus.

"For this reason I will not be negligent to remind you always of these things, though you know and are established in the present truth. Yes, I thing it is right, as long as I am in this tent, to stir you up by reminding you, knowing that shortly I must put off my tent just as our Lord Jesus Christ showed me. Moreover, I will be careful to ensure that you always have a reminder of these things after my decease." **Vs. 12 – 15**

These believers that Peter is writing have been taught, have been given training and they knew the Scriptures. But here is the danger of the believer who has been taught, trained and led in the Christian life; the believer can become haughty, proud and overconfident in their Christian life. In **1 Corinthians 10:12** Paul gives a similar warning: *"Therefore let him who thinks he stands take heed lest he fall."* It seems as though the more successful a believer become in his Christian life the more likely he is to think that he has it all together and can handle things by himself. At this point he is an unconscious incompetent.

Someone has made this cycle of a believers life that is displayed in the life of Moses: At first he began to take things in his own hands thinking because he was a prince in Egypt he could avenge his people and he killed an Egyptian soldier. He took those actions because he was a unconscious incompetent, he didn't know he was incompetent. Because of those actions he was run out of Egypt to the wilderness for 40 years. At this point of his life he became a conscious incompetent. Moses knew he was incompetent to do what God had called him to do at this time.

During those 40 years of training Moses became an unconscious competent. God called him at the burning bush but Moses was frightened because of earlier failures in his life. As Moses obeyed he soon came to understand that he was competent to do what God had called him to do because of the power of God displayed in his life. At this point Moses was a conscious competent.

Now Moses had a danger in his life that was displayed at the Rock in **Numbers 20:11 &12** and his authority went to his head and he thought he was more capable than he was and he sinned by doing more than God asked him to do. *". . . Because you did not believe Me, to hallow Me in the eyes of the children of Israel, therefore you shall not bring the assembly into the land which I have given them."* **NKJV**

Moses fell again because he though he was competent but he was not; he began the cycle once more, he returned to be an <u>unconscious incompetent</u>. This is what Peter is warning the believers about; be careful, take heed because you are in danger of falling; they needed to be reminded and reminded frequently. This is the purpose of his writing this book. Peter knew he would die soon and with that knowledge and the understanding of the church, he would leave them a written reminder.

There are two cautions here; one is that people need to be reminded of what is important in life and they need to be reminded frequently; the other is that leaders need to be diligent to remind people frequently. I think this caution is also a challenge to fathers, mothers, grandfathers and grandmothers to leave with their children and grandchildren a written reminder that can be read well after they have died.

Peter uses the word *"tent"* in the **New King James Version** and the idea of a tent is a temporary dwelling. We are sojourners and pilgrims here on this earth, we are just traveling through on our way to our eternal home in heaven. This *"tent"* will ware out, and we will fade away but heaven, our new home and new body will not.

Peter tells the reader that although they may be "established" in the truth, they must be reminded constantly about the truth that they have been established.

"For we did not follow cunningly devised fables when we made known to you the power and coming of our Lord Jesus Christ, but were eyewitnesses of His majesty." **Vs. 16**

This faith that Peter is teaching is not something that was humanly thought up and fashioned into a cunningly arranged tale. Peter and the Apostles were actually eyewitnesses of all that Jesus did while on this earth. They personally saw with their own eyes what took place. They experience the presence of Jesus and felt the power of His majesty.

"For He received from God the Father honor and glory when such a voice came to Him from the Excellent Glory: 'This is My beloved Son, in whom I am well pleased.' And we heard this voice which came from heaven when we were with on the holy mountain." **Vs. 17 & 18**

Peter, James and John did not hear about the voice of the Father, they actually heard for themselves, the voice of God the Father. The Father confirmed to them the validity of what Jesus had been telling them, that He was the Son of God, we now have God the Father, *"the Excellent Glory"* personally spoking to them.

The Father was well pleased in "all" that His Son Jesus did. It reminds me of what God said after his creation work was done, *"Then God saw everything that He had made, and indeed it was very good* (well pleasing), " **Genesis 1:31 NKJV** .

"And so we have the prophetic word confirmed, which you do well to heed as a light that shines in a dark place, until the day dawn and the morning star rises in your hearts; knowing this first, that no prophecy of Scripture is of any private interpretation, for prophecy never came by the will of man, but holy men of God spoke as they were moved by the holy Spirit." **Vs. 19 & 20**

So, we have the personal voice of God the Father confirming to Peter, James and John that Jesus is who He said He was and we also have the Scriptures which have prophesied of Jesus. The Scripture was not fashioned by the mind of man. Scripture is inspired of God, and comes by those whom He inspired to write. Scripture came from God's Holy Spirit through those men He chose to write to man for us to read.

The proofs of authenticity are:
1. God the Father
2. God the Son
3. The eyewitness of the disciple and apostles
4. The writings of Scripture.

Anything other than these has no credibility. Anything other than these four is false and not true.

Chapter 2

"But there were also false prophets among the people, even as there will be false teachers among you, who will secretly bring in destructive heresies, even denying the Lord who bought them, and bring on themselves swift destruction. And many will follow their destructive ways, because of whom the way of truth will be blasphemed." **Vs. 1 & 2**

A false prophet is a person who claims to be a prophet of God but he is not. A false teacher is a person who claims to be a teacher of the Scripture but does not. A false prophet or teacher will proclaim and teach false truths. What they preach or teach is something close to The Truth but it is in actuality, a lie.

When a person goes to the court, the judge has that person to take an oath, to confirm or to promise or to swear that everything he says, every answer he gives will be only truth, not tainted or expressed in any way that would cause someone to think what he said is something other than, pure and complete truth. To give added strength to the promise, the court bailiff will bring a Bible and ask the witness to place his or her right hand upon the Bible (The Truth of God) and then to raise the other hand up before all to ask the help of God with the answers and to confirm to the court that what he or she is about to say is "the truth, the whole truth and nothing but the truth".

For something to be "the truth" in must contain all the truth and have within in nothing but the truth in order to be "nothing but the truth". A lawyer will try to "taint" the truth to be something other than the truth by the way the lawyer asks the question and so that lawyer is asking for a lie. That lawyer is asking for a response that might causer a Juror to believe a tainted truth or should I say, to believe a carefully fashioned lie. The lawyer becomes a false teacher, he or she is teaching a lie.

The caution for the believer is that in the church there "will be" people who "sneak " into a fellowship of believers with the intent to "mislead" or to teach something other than The Truth or Scripture. There specific purpose is to "lead away" the unsuspecting believer. The results of this misleading is to bring doubt or confusion to the believers life in Christ. The confused believer will not lose his salvation but his life becomes a life of uncertainty, unfruitfulness, and fear and he has lost or longer has that joy of his salvation that he once had. This is the fruit of a lie, brought about by a false prophet or false teacher. God's punishment of these false prophets and false teachers will be swift destruction and eternal destruction. That is an awful thought but a just punishment for false teaching, making the Truth misunderstood and making it a lie.

Peter is saying that we should not accept what someone teaches or preaches as being the truth based solely upon the fact that they are likeable people. Reliability is something that has been proven to be reliable and proven that it is trustworthy. It is earned and not an entitlement.

These teachers will even lead the unsuspecting student to the point that they would question God Himself. Be careful of these people!

"By covetousness they will exploit you with deceptive words; for a long time their judgment has not been idle, and their destruction does not slumber." **Vs. 3**

The purpose of these people, these false teachers is greed. There desire is not to make you a better person but to make you a poorer person; they come to get your money or to benefit from your misplaced trust that you have placed upon them. They will exploit, rob and destroy your life. Jesus told his disciples that *"The thief come to steal, kill and destroy. I came that they may have life and have it abundantly."* **John 10:10 ESV**

These false teachers do not quit easily, they work hard and they will not sleep until they achieve their purpose in destroying your life completely. Be careful of these people!

The good news is that these false teachers do not fool God; they have not escaped God's judgment upon them for their deeds. Their destruction will be swift when the time comes. God's judgment is calculated and it will be just and complete.

"it is a fearful thing to fall into the hands of a living God." **Hebrews 10:31 NKJV**

"And there is no creature hidden from His sight, but all things are naked and open to the eyes of Him to whom we must give account." **Hebrews 4:13 NKJV**

God is not slow, God is faithful and He is sure in what He does. God's moving is not affected by the opinion of man or any other creation. God has His plan and He works His plan in His way and according to His schedule that does not change. God cannot change because there is nothing that He does not know and He gets it right the first time.

Someone might say: What about Satan? To that I must say: What about Satan? I am not Creator God nor are you. I do not know the mind of God and neither do you. I believe God is God and I am not so I follow Him with confidence, I do not turn to the right or to the left in unbelief, I do not wish to stray from following Him. I often have strayed but He drew me back. I will follow Him until I die and believe Him throughout eternity.

The creature creation of the Creator cannot fathom the mind of the Creator, he can only trust; and so I trust. You also must trust and follow Him not the false teachers that you know. I don't have to know the answer to everything I only need to trust and follow Him Who knows everything.

"For if God did not spare the angels who sinned, but cast them down to hell and delivered them into chains of darkness, to be reserved for judgment; and did not spare the ancient world, but saved Noah, one of eight people, preacher of righteousness, bringing in the flood on the world of ungodly; and turned the cities of Sodom and Gomorrah into ashes, condemned them to destruction, making them an example to those who afterward would live ungodly;" **Vs. 4 – 6**

The believer should not question the schedule of God's judgment by the life line of their own life. Judgment will come as sure as there is a God in heaven. God has spoken to us through His Word and revealed to us a warning against rebellion and unfaithfulness. We must believe, we must trust and we must obey His Word without any action of unbelief.

Judgment for the angels has not been fulfilled yet, they are being held in chains of darkness right now awaiting their judgment. The rebellious angels of Satan and Satan himself, have not escaped God's judgment upon them; they are reserved for judgment.

Judgment came to the world in Noah's time. Noah preached righteousness but the unrighteous would have none of it and they turned their ear away, they turned their dying ear away. All but eight people died!

Judgment came to the citizens of Sodom and to the citizens of Gomorrah because of their unspeakable depravity. A depravity and judgment that stands out today as a warning of judgment from God for such depravity.

Judgment will come to the unbelieving and disobedient people today. This is the warning of God and this is the command of God. We should never wonder if God is overlooking the sins of people today; He has not nor will He overlook any sin.

"And delivered righteous Lot, who was oppressed by the filthy conduct of the wicked (for that righteous man, dwelling among them, tormented his righteous soul from day to day by seeing and hearing their lawless deeds)-then

the Lord knows how to deliver the godly out of temptations and to reserve the unjust under punishment for the day of judgment, and especially those who walk according to the flesh in the lust of uncleanness and despise authority. They are presumptuous, self-willed. They are not afraid to speak evil of dignitaries, where as angels, who are greater in power and might, do not bring a reviling accusation against them before the Lord." **Vs. 7 – 11**

God's judgment for evil is sure but His "delivering" hand from evil is also sure and is to be always trusted, under all circumstances. Paul writes in **1 Corinthians 10:13** *"No temptation has overtaken you except such as is common to man; but God is faithful, who will not allow you to be tempted beyond what you are able, but with the temptation will also make a way of escape, that you may be able to bear it."* **NKJV** Again, God is not inattentive, God is sure. God knows how to deliver, do not lose heart.

The nephew of Abraham is Lot and we have many preconceived ideas of Lot therefore many believers with preconceived ideas have a difficulty reading this adjective that is given to Lot here: *"righteous Lot"*. Lot was living in a wicked place, Lot was there because of a personal choice he had made in his younger life when he separated from his uncle Abraham. Abraham is the one who understood that it was time for Lot to move on and He gave Lot the choice. **Genesis 13:10 & 11** *"And Lot lifted his eyes and saw all the plain of Jordan, that it was well watered everywhere (before the Lord destroyed Sodom and Gomorrah) like the garden of the Lord, like the land of Egypt as you go toward Zoar. Then Lot chose for himself all the plain of Jordan, and Lot journeyed east. And they separated from each other."* **NKJV**

Was the choice of Lot a righteous choice? A righteous choice is a good choice for all concerned; it is a choice that is beneficial for everyone. Was Lot's choice of a place of residence a good choice? Perhaps he was a representative of righteousness within the unrighteousness of the people there. I really do not know the right answer here, I only know that we have that descriptive adjective associated with Lot here, and placed here under the moving of the Holy Spirit upon Peter to refer to Lot as "righteous Lot".

So, taking this scripture as inspired, I must also call Lot righteous. With that understanding the next reference to Lot is that his "righteous soul" was greatly bothered by the conduct of the citizens of those cities. Lot's eyes and ears were greatly troubled; he didn't like what he was hearing nor did he approve of what he saw. The passage leads us on to understand that Lot thought about his situation continually night and day. Lot needed deliverance for sure and the confidence here is that though Lot was *"tormented"* by the situation and did not know what to do but God already knew how to deliver Lot and how he was going to unleash judgment upon the cities.

The believer today also finds himself trouble, confused and tormented by the conduct of our world, and we search for an answer as to what we might do and how we should respond. The answer for us is the same as it was in Lot's time and that is that God already knows what to do and how He will work; therefore, we only need to do what God asks of us to do and when we should do it. Keep your eyes open, keep your ears in tune with the Holy Spirit and be quick to respond to His leading.

God's judgment is sure. He has already judged the fallen angels; He has already judged the pre-flood people; He has already judged the cities of Sodom and Gomorrah and God is going to judge them and the rest of the world at the Great White Throne Judgment. **Revelation 20:11 – 15**

God's deliverance is also sure. If He could deliver Lot in the situation he was in He can deliver us as well in the situation that we find ourselves. The believer is not judged at the Great White Throne Judgment but rather, at the "Bema" or the "Judgment Seat of Christ".   (**2 Corinthians 5:10** *"For we must all appear before the Judgment Seat of Christ, that each one may receive the things done in the body, according to what he has done, whether, good or bad,"* **NKJV**); It is there, the Judgment Seat of Christ, where the believer will receive rewards for faithful service and where reward will be taken away because of not being diligent and faithful in service. Our reward will be determined by how we lived and how valuable or significant to the cause of Christ those deeds were. Some were most valuable and many were of less significance. Paul relates to the reader, to be made of gold, silver, precious stone, wood, hay or stubble **1 Corinthians 3:12 – 17**

There are degrees of punishment in hell and God is especially hard upon those who are more grievous in their lives against humanity and against God Himself. **Luke 12:47 & 48** *And that servant who knew his master's will, and did not prepare himself or do according to his will, shall be beaten with many stripes. But he who did not know, yet committed things deserving of stripes, shall be beaten with few. For everyone to whom much is given,* *from him much will be required; and to whom much has been committed, of him they will ask the more."* **NKJV**

The truth is that hell was prepared for Satan and his angels but the disobedient will go there in punishment for refusing the gift of God, the gift of eternal life and their reward is the wage of eternal death in Hell with Satan and his angels. **Matthew 25:41 – 46**

"Of how much worse punishment, do you suppose, will he be thought worthy who has trampled the Son of God underfoot, counted the blood of the covenant b which he was sanctified a common thing, and insulted the Sprit of grace? For we know him who said, 'Vengeance is mine, I will repay,' says the Lord, and again, 'The Lord will judge His people, it is a fearful thing to fall into the hands of the living God.'" **Hebrews 10:29 – 31 NKJV**

Remember, God hates pride, arrogance, self-willed and scoffers of those in authority. Dignitaries or "glorious one" in some translations are those whom God has placed for His purposes, to be used at His commands. With this understanding we must be careful to speak evil of them. Peter notes that the angels of heaven who are more knowledgeable and much more powerful that human beings do not slander earthly dignitaries. Angels never question the movement of God they respond to the voice of God and that is what we must do. We must respond to God as He bids us to respond.

"But these, like natural brute beast made to be caught and destroyed, speak evil of the things they do not understand and will utterly perish in their own corruption, and will receive the wages of unrighteousness, as those who count it pleasure to carouse in the daytime. They are

spots and blemishes, carousing in their own deceptions while they feast with you, having eyes full of adultery and that cannot cease form sin, enticing unstable souls. They have a heart trained in covetous practices and are accursed children." **Vs. 12 – 14**

The false teacher is compared to vicious animals on this earth. They do not think correctly, they just merely react to the idea of "survival of the fittest". For them their lives is a "dog eat dog" world in their mind. They are out to get what they can before someone else gets what they can from them. They have no love for others above the love they have for themselves. They plot and scheme to get ahead. They laugh at authority, and lord themselves over all that they can. These wicked people are bold in their sinning; they live to sin and to do increasingly greater sin throughout life. Paul writes of this type of people in **Romans 1:24 – 32**.

To the believer, it seems as though they are getting away with their crimes and sins but they are not, their judgment awaits them as sure as Jesus is coming back for us.

"They have forsaken the right way and gone astray, following the way of Balaam the son of Beor, who loved the wages of unrighteousness. But he was rebuked for his iniquity: a dumb donkey speaking with a man's voice restrained the madness of the prophet." **VS. 15 & 16**

"The wages of unrighteousness" means that they love and live for money or anything that might bring them personal profit. They know better but love themselves more than anyone.

The example of the prophet Balaam in **Numbers 22 – 31:8** is used here to describe the character of these false teachers. Balaam loved money and that love for money caused him to develop a life that brought him profit not character and love for God. It is noteworthy here to notice that Peter calls them *"bruit beast"* and notes that it was a beast of burden, a *"dumb donkey speaking with a man's voice"* to shake him.

"These are wells without water, clouds carried by a tempest, for whom is reserved the blackness of darkness forever." **VS. 17**

These people know of God and His desire for man but although they know it, they reject it. A well that has no water is only a hole in the ground. A cloud that contains water but is blown away by the wind before it can drop the much needed life sustaining water to the ground and only leaves a mist in the air is a storm, it contains the substance of things that was hoped for but leaves no substance at all. The cloud that is carried away by the wind cause fear because of the storm and the cloud itself blackens the sun and leaves us hopeless.

"For when they speak great swelling words of emptiness, they allure through the lusts of the flesh, through lewdness, the ones who have actually escaped from those who lie in error." **Vs. 18**

This is the example of a false prophet and false teacher. These false teachers have a bloated opinion of themselves and they often flaunt a lavish lifestyle and to create envy and deception of others. They promise great things, they proclaim freedom, prosperity, good health, a pain-free life, power and knowledge but when all is said and done, there is nothing but fear and hopelessness left. Their goal is to trap, enslave others to the wickedness of the world that the Good News delivers them from. God's judgment for these people is the darkest part of hell and greater darkness for all eternity. God is not fooled by the false teacher, though they fool many; the judgment of God upon them is not hindered, lessened or escapable. God's punishment upon these dissenters and promoters of a lie is most grievous for sure. Woe, to them!

"While they promise them liberty, they themselves are slaves of corruption, for by whom a person is overcome, by him also he is brought into bondage, for if, after they have escaped the pollutions of the world through the knowledge of the Lord and Savior Jesus Christ, they are again entangled in them and over come, the latter end is worse for them that the beginning. For it would be better for them not to have known the way of righteousness, than having known it, to turn from the holy commandment delivered to them. But it has happened to them according to the true proverb: 'A dog returns to his own vomit, and the sow having washed, to her wallowing in the mire.' " **Vs. 19 – 22**

False teachers are actually slaves themselves; they are totally controlled by the evil desires that they promote. The sad truth here is the unsuspecting students of these false teachers once were freed from the pull of the world because of the Truth that they had been taught but now have been drawn back into a worse lifestyle and held with a tighter grip. They now find themselves sunk lower into the captivity of various sins and worse off than before.

Peter makes the notation that it would have been better for them if they had not been enlightened in the first place. Their life would not have been a depraved as it is now under the teaching of these false teachers. He uses a proverb to illustrate this and the objects used here are a dog and a pig; two of the most detestable animals for the Jewish and middle-eastern area. No one wanted to be compared to a dog or pig. No one wants to be in this situation; so, the caution is given.

Chapter 3

"Beloved, I now write to you this second epistle (in both of which I stir up your pure minds by way of reminder.) that you may be mindful of the words which were spoken before by the holy prophets, and of the commandments of us, the apostles of the Lord and Savior." **Vs. 1 & 2**

This is the second letter by Peter to the scattered church and the purpose of both of them is to serve as a lasting reminder for troubling times that were to come. Peter wants them to be alert and to try the spirits of those teachers to see if they are genuine. John also cautioned in his letter: *"Beloved, do not believe every spirit, but test the spirits, whether they are of God; because many false prophets have gone out into the world. By this you know the Spirit of God: Every spirit that confesses that Jesus Christ has come in the flesh is of God, and every sprit that does not confess that Jesus Christ has come in the flesh is not of God. And this is the spirit of the Antichrist, which you have heard was coming, and is now already in the world."* **1 John 4:1 – 3 NKJV**

It is of supreme importance that the believer follow only the true teaching of Scripture. There are preachers and teachers of Scripture who pervert the pure word. Be on the watch, be careful and test those teachers and preachers.

Another caution for today is that there is no new scripture, no new teaching other than the Bible. The Bible is the authority, Jesus is the content of the Bible and Jesus is the Gospel or Good News which the believer is commanded by Jesus to be its carrier to the world. The Holy Spirit is the teacher, the informer and its translator.

Be a student and scholar of the Word. Here is a good foundational tool in your study of Scripture: *"The task of the scholar is guarantee the purity of the text to get as close as possible to the Word as originally given. He may compare Scripture with Scripture until he discovers the true meaning of the text. But he must never sit in judgment, upon what is written, he must not bring the meaning of the Word before the bar of his reason."* **Found written in the front of my Dad's Bible**

"Knowing this first: that scoffers will come in the last days, walking according to their own lusts, and saying, 'Where is the promise of His coming? For since the fathers fell asleep, all things continue as they were from the beginning of creation.' For this they willfully forget: that by the word of God the heavens were of old, and the earth standing out of water and in the water, by which the world that then existed perished, being flooded with water. But the heavens and the earth which now exist are kept in store by the same word, reserved for fire until the day of judgment and perdition of ungodly men." **Vs. 3 – 7**

No teacher, preacher or professor deserves your trust; always test, question and be skeptical of the teachings and "opinions" of others. Remember people are just people and people can be and have been wrong. The Holy Sprit is God and He cannot be wrong and He is the Teacher that Jesus has appointed as our Instructor.

"However, when the Spirit of Truth has come, He will guide you into all truth; for He will not speak on His own authority, but whatever He hears He will speak; and He will tell you things to come. He will glorify Me, for He will take of what is Mine and declare it to you." **John 16:13 & 14 NKJV**

Peter heard of scoffers in his day, Jesus had scoffers that opposed Him and there continue to be scoffers today. Scoffers will increase as time goes on and their lineage or heritage of scoffing will not change. They scoff because they oppose God; they scoff because they are the voice of Satan. Satan is the prince and power of the air we read **Ephesians 2:2** that works in the sons of disobedience. The sons of disobedience are his prophets, preachers and teachers. Expect them for they are among us. Our war is not against flesh and blood Paul writes in **Ephesians 6:12** it is against principalities and powers of Satan. They are all around us, so look for them, expect them.

The battle cry of the scoffers is: *"So, where is Jesus? I though He was supposed to come back. He did say He was, didn't He?"* Yep, it is the same-ol'-same-ol'. The mind set of these scoffers is they do not want to know anything other than what they want to know. I call that "Preferred Ignorance". They prefer ignorance or as Peter says here *"they willfully forget"* or they conveniently forget that God is the Creator of all things and He is sovereign.

In **Genesis 1:6 – 10** we have the account of creation. We read here that God sandwiched the firmament, the expanse or heaven of earth between the "waters above the firmament and waters below the firmament." What happened is a water shield of protection from the

163

sunrays and caused the earth to be an even temperature in all places. He also placed the waters or seas (**Job 38:10 & 11** *"when I fixed My limit for it, and set bars and doors; when I said, 'This far you may come, but no farther, and her your proud waves must stop!'"* **NKJV from** the ground and the seas "under the earth' or underground rivers below the earth. These waters were unleashed in God's judgment on the earth as we read in **Genesis 7:11** *"In the six hundredth year of Noah's life, in the second month, the seventeenth day of the month, on that day all the fountains of the great deep were broken up, and the windows of heaven were opened. And the rain was on the earth forty days and forty nights."* **NKJV**

People didn't believe God's Word preached through Noah in those days, they didn't believe Jesus, they rejected the Word preached in the early church and they do not believe God's Word today; nothing has changed. The pre-flood earth was reserved for destruction by water in the days of Noah and it will be destroyed by fire in the last days; the "same-ol'-same-ol". People still scoff as they did in the time of the great flood in Noah's days.

"But beloved, do not forget this one thing, that with the Lord one day is as a thousand years, and a thousand years as one day." **Vs. 8**

Peter encourages the believer, when the scoffers ridicule you for believing God Word and His promise, don't be discouraged because God is not bound by time but He is bound to His "Timing". Time doesn't mean anything to a God that does not exist in the boundaries of time. God is "timeless" He is faithful to His Word and cannot be unfaithful.

164

What is a thousand year to an eternal God? It is nothing.

"The Lord is not slack concerning His promise, as some count slackness, but is longsuffering toward us not willing that any should perish but that all should come to repentance." **Vs. 9**

God never slows down his will, His desires, His plan; He works His plan in His "timing". We alter our plans because of events and situations that come up but nothing just comes up to God, nothing surprises Him, nothing "just accurse" to God; God never leaves anything out because He is "all Knowing". All knowing means there is nothing that can be known but that God does not know it or was there ever a time when He did not know it. There is no time with God because He is eternal. God is, God always was and God will always be. I cannot understand that because I am not God. I have to yield to God's all knowingness when I cannot understand.

You may ask yourself: Why doesn't God just go ahead and destroy this earth? Well, the reason is that because God knows all, he knows every human being that has lived on this earth, all who are on the earth right now and all who will ever live on this earth before it is destroyed. Having all this understanding of humanity he is patient and He gives every creation every opportunity to turn to Him. When a person dies without Christ Jesus they will be totally guilty of rejecting God. Every person will have more than sufficient time and opportunity to turn to Christ Jesus. The young, the old and all in between that reject Him will have no excuse. That is why God waits, that is why He is long suffering *"toward us"* He does not want even one person to die without repenting. The sad thing is that many do die without repenting and trample under their foot the patience and kindness of God.

"But the day of the Lord will come as a thief in the night, in which the heavens will pass away with a great noise, and the elements will melt with fervent heat; both the earth and the works that are in it will be burned up." **Vs. 10**

Bad news! God is patient but His patience will one day end. That day is called "the day of the Lord". That day will be a day of unexpectedness and unpreparedness by many. That day will come like a thief will come. The thief comes in his timing, he comes when you are least expecting and he comes to kill, steal and destroy Jesus told his disciples.

In that day, the day of the Lord, that day will be as no other; the melting of the elements of life, the planets of the universe, the sun, the moon and the stars of this vast universe will explode with a great noise an a great heat, fire from God and all that has ever been will be no more. What a day that will be and that will be a day that I do not want to be evolved in on while on this earth.

The Good News is that you do not have to be a recipient of God's wrath, you can experience in its place the love, joy, peace, gentleness, kindness, grace and mercy of God. Who would choose judgment I want to thing. But the truth is that most people will choose judgment because of accepting the lie of Satan.

"Nevertheless we, according to His promise look for new heavens and a new earth in which righteousness dwells." **Vs. 13**

Yes, this is the other choice, the choice of God and to be a recipient of His grace and mercy. To receive a new heaven, to live on a new earth and within a New Jerusalem to worship Him. **Revelation 21;1 – 3** To be able to live with God and surrounded by and with His righteousness; no more unrighteousness all of that will be a thing of the past and never to be thought of through out all eternity. There will not be any remembrance of evil or bad times because all things will be made new, no sorrow, no crying and no more pain. What a wonderful place to be and you can be there. All you need to do is to accept Jesus Christ as your Savior. If you repent of your sin and begin a new life in Jesus Christ, heaven is your reward. If you refuse then you will receive the wage for your sin and that wages of sin is death. *"For the wages of sin is death, but the gift of God is eternal life in Christ Jesus our Lord."* **Romans 6:23 NKJV**

"Therefore, beloved, looking forward to these things, be diligent to be found by Him in peace, without spot and blameless;" **Vs. 14**

Now that you know and understand that Jesus is coming back and it will be in a moment that we are not expecting him to come it behooves all believers to be very proactive, purposeful and aggressive in our daily living to be all that Jesus desires for us to be. Though we are looking forward to His coming with great eagerness, our mission is not complete yet. If we are diligent in spreading the Good News then we will be at peace in our living and certain that at the moment that Jesus does come we will be found without blame in our mission that was given to us by Jesus Himself. We will be ready.

"And consider that the longsuffering of our Lord is salvation-as also our beloved brother Paul, according to the wisdom given to him, has written to your, as also in all his epistles, speaking in them of these things, in some things hard to understand, which untaught and unstable people twist to their own destruction, as they do also the rest of the Scriptures." **Vs. 15 & 16**

The purpose for the *"longsuffering"* of God is displayed in His kindness and goodness; which Paul wrote of in **Romans 2:4** *"Or do you despise the riches of His goodness, forbearance, and longsuffering not knowing that the goodness of God leads you to repentance?"* **NKJV**

Yes, God is not willing that anyone at all should perish and so He is longsuffering, God is patient and God is kind toward mankind. God gives every person, every opportunity to turn to Him. To truly believe in Jesus is to repent of your wrong direction in which you have been living your life. Repentance is turning around. God's longsuffering gives time for repentance and repentance leads to salvation.

Peter gives recognition to the Apostle Paul's Epistles or letters that he wrote to the churches and believers in Christ Jesus where he told of the coming again of Christ. Peter also reminds the reader that the false teachers and false preachers of the day will always do all that they can to confuse those who will listen to them. I might remind you also that in this day there are many false teachers and false preachers who are perverting Scripture. The believer MUST try the spirits of all teachers and preachers to see if they are true representations of The Truth. *"Beloved, do not believe every spirit, but test the spirits, whether they are of God; because many false prophets have gone out into the world."* **1 John 4:1 NKJV**

A false teacher or preacher is someone who is taught to teach in stealth or in an unsuspecting way; so be careful, test all. These teachers and prophets seem to be right but not right. If you ever have a eerie feeling about someone, take caution because that eerie feeling may be there because the Holy Spirit has placed it there. Always test things; no one deserves the "benefit of the doubt" when it comes to Scripture.

Truth never has to be twisted; Truth is truth and is not be twisted to fit the doctrine of anyone. Scripture rests in Scripture. The authority of Scripture is Scripture itself because it is the Word of God Himself. God alone is to be trusted *". . . let God be true but every man a liar. . ."* **Romans 3:4 NKJV**

False prophets, preachers and teachers have always been around and they will continue to be found everywhere, even in your own church and circle of believers; they are there so, expect them, test them and rest in the Holy Spirit to reveal them to you; but you must first test them.

You therefore, beloved, since you know this beforehand, beware lest you also fall from your own steadfastness, being led away with the error of the wicked." **Vs. 17**

As we read here in **2 Peter 3:17** Paul also warns the believer in **1 Corinthians 10:12** *"Therefore let him who things he stands take heed lest he fall."* **NKJV** A believer never gets to the point that he is above falling or being led away from the Truth into the clutches of false

169

teaching and doctrine. A believer must TEST all teachings to see if they are of God.

The purpose of false teaching and doctrine is to destroy, those teachers are "wicked"; they are not of God, they are of Satan! Remember this at all times and in every place.

"but grow in the grace and knowledge of our Lord and Savior Jesus Christ. To Him be the glory both now and forever. Amen.

Peter concludes this second Epistle, this second letter with a doxology. Peter's desire, his prayer and his aim for what he has written is to produce growth in the believers; he wants the grace and knowledge that they presently have to increase, to flower and produce fruit and new growth of new believers. Peter wants the readers to be found faithful to the ministry of spreading the Good News to the whole world and to make disciples who will in turn make disciples. That is the meaning of the Great Commission given to Peter and us by our Lord Jesus Christ. **Matthew 28:18 - 20** *"And Jesus came and spoke to them, saying, 'All authority has been given to Me in heaven and on earth. Go therefore and make disciples of all the nations, baptizing them in the name of the Father and of the Son and of the Holy Spirit, teaching them to observe all things that I have commanded you, and lo, I am with you always, even to the end of the age. Amen.'"* **NKJV**

The final admonition is that Jesus must be the recipient of all praise and glory in all that we do. It is not about me, it is all about: Him and them as Jesus answered the false religious leaders in **Matthew 22:34 – 40** *".. you shall love the Lord your God with all your heart, with all* *your soul and with all your mind. This is the first and great commandment. And the second is like it: You shall love your neighbor as yourself . . . "* **NKJV**

"You are worthy, O Lord, to receive glory and honor and power; for You created all things, and by Your will they exist and were created." **Revelation 4:11 NKJV**

Yes, He alone deserved glory, honor and power for all time and eternity! To this the only thing left to say is: *Amen!* And with that Peter closes his Epistle or letter.

Just the Basics

Discovering the Truth in an Untruthful World

Commentary on First John, Second John and Third John

By
Danny Glenn Thomas

Introduction

Learning the Truth;
Recognizing the Truth;
Living out the Truth
in an untruthful world.

The early church had many problems with those who would change the Good News to something that resembled the religious group that they had come out of. Two major problems were those known as the Judaizers who desired to inject elements of the Law into the grace that Jesus proclaimed. The Judaizers would have their gentile listeners add to the work of Christ, works of the Law as a requirement of God's Salvation. The Jerusalem Counsel in **Acts 15** dealt with this matter of mixing Judaism with Christianity.

The second major group causing confusion in the early church was the Gnostics. The Gnostics came out of a Greek influence, relating a special knowledge with the Good News. Gnosticism was steeped in pride for human knowledge, understanding and reasoning and they applied it to this new found Good News of Christ Jesus; they were known as the Gnostics. They believed in a dualism doctrine denying that spirit and material could co-exist in one body. They believed creation had two separate elements one flesh or material and the other spirit. They believed that matter or material substance was evil and that only the spirit was good. They believed that mankind was lost because of his imprisonment in a material body and that his only hope of salvation was through self-knowledge. They denied the incarnation of Jesus in that his body was matter and that good and evil could not be in one body. They taught that Jesus was born as a human being and that after he died on the cross, at that point the Divine Spirit of God came upon him and He became God. They were mixing Greek wisdom, reasoning and thought of the day with the Good News of Jesus, this new Christianity they had discovered. The Gnostic felt that only a few were given this knowledge and that after they had received that special knowledge they were free to live as they wished. They felt that they were superior to others. This is the Gnostic Gospel.

Still today we have those who want to say a person is not saved unless he does certain things in his life. The results this false doctrine of works creates a defeated believer, living a life of uncertainty and never actually sure of their salvation. They are captive to the doctrine of other people and seeking the approval of that gospel as an affirmation of their salvation. We also have those who feel they are above the cautions of Scripture and are free to live as he wishes.

John restates the Gospel of Jesus in his epistles or letters. He strongly confirms the divinity of Jesus, His love for man and His work of redemption. The message is that a person is born of God by believing that Jesus is the only begotten Son of God and that it was the personal work of Jesus that secures that salvation.

John emphasizes that the believer must desire to live a righteous life with Jesus as our model and that we should want to seek Him and obey Him. John strongly promotes the love of God for His children and the significance of the believers love for others. The icon of the believer is the love of God displayed in his life and that love is how he is distinguished from all others of the world.

John was the beloved disciple and one of the inner circle of Peter, James and John.

Chapter One

"That which was from the beginning, which we have heard, which we have seen with our eyes, which we have looked upon, and our hands have handled, concerning the Word of life-" **Vs. 1**

John establishes his credibility here. What he is about to say is from a first hand eyewitness account. He did not hear this from someone else, he heard it personally from the mouth of Jesus; he saw these things with his own eyes, he was there when that happened. He knew Jesus, he was with Jesus and he had physical contact with Jesus. He touched Jesus, He talked with Jesus in a one on one situation.

"the life was manifested, and we have seen, and bear witness and declare to you that eternal life which as with the Father and was manifested to us-that which we have seen and heard we declare to you, that you also may have fellowship with us; and truly our fellowship is with the Father and with His Son Jesus Christ. And these things we write to you that your joy may be full." **Vs. 2,3 & 4**

God the Father is the one who sent His Son Jesus to the world to be their Savior. The angel told Joseph to call the baby Jesus which means Savior because He would be the Savior of mankind. **Luke 1:13** *"And behold you will conceive n your womb and bring for a Son, and shall call His name Jesus."* **Matthew 1:20 & 21** *". . . Joseph, son of*

179

David, do not be afraid to take to you Mary your wife, for that which is conceived in her is of the Holy Spirit, and she will bring forth a Son, and you shall call His name Jesus, for He will save His people from their sins." **NKJV**

He was God with us or Emmanuel **Matthew 1:23** and Mary asked: *"How can this be?"* **Luke 1:34 The** response can only be: *"For with God nothing will be impossible."* **Luke 1:37 Jesus** was all God and all man, Son of God; son of man. Mary was the human vehicle through which Jesus was born of man as the son of man and the Holy Spirit, proceeding from the Father, was the God part bringing about the conception, to be the God part. Therefore, Jesus was to be born as God through man or God with us, Emmanuel.

"And the angel answered and said to her, The Holy Spirit will come upon you and the power of the Highest will overshadow you therefore also, the Holy One Who is to be born will be called the Son of God." **Luke 1:35 NKJV**

"Do you not believe that I am in the Father, and the Father in Me? The words that I speak to you I do not speak on My own authority: but the Father Who dwells in Me does the works. Believe Me that I am in the Father and the Father in me, or else believe Me for the sake of the works themselves." **John 14:10 & 11 NKJV**

"I and My Father are one." **John 10:30 NKJV**

John is declaring Jesus as the Son of God once again; he is reaffirming the truth of the Gospel to the believer. John wants the reader and listener to see Jesus as the Son of God sent to man to redeem him and become his Savior. This understanding will give them the joy of knowing for certain that they are sons of God and purpose in life and passion in spreading the Good News to others. This understanding will help them to refute the opposition that they will encounter and be able to resist that opposition in the church.

"This is the message which we have heard from Him and declare to you, that God is light and in Him is no darkness at all." **Vs. 5**

This is similar to the beginning of the Gospel of John *"In the beginning was the Word, and the Word was with God, and the Word was God. He was in the beginning with God. All things were made through Him, and without Him nothing was made that was made. In Him was life and the life was the light of men. And the light shines in the darkness and the darkness did not comprehend it."* **John 1:1 – 5 NKJV**

Light brings understanding, light corrects error and light dispels any darkness at all. Jesus is light and where Jesus is there can be no darkness. The understanding here that John is giving to the reader is that he has authority to write and declare to them what he has seen and what he has heard. John is saying that he is declaring to them that light that he saw without any shadow of turning from the truth. John is about to give to them the truth, the whole truth and nothing but the truth. And the truth is that Jesus is The Truth and in that Truth there is no darkness at all. You can depend on what you hear and read as being the genuine Truth of God.

If we say that we have fellowship with Him, and walk in darkness, we lie and do not practice the truth. But if we walk in the light as He is in the light, we have fellowship with one another, and the blood of Jesus Christ His Son cleanses us from all sin." **Vs. 6 & 7**

181

Light is what the Gnostics were teaching; teaching that they had light and those believers who were not of their group were to be ostracized. That is a good word to use here because an ostrich is known for hiding from impending danger by hiding their head in the sand. Darkness does not take danger away; darkness increases danger. Jesus wants to give us His light that is the Truth. His light and truth makes all the difference in life. With light, we see truth and having seen the Truth we can practice the Truth with confidence. Light brings about fellowship with one another, we see others clearly and enjoy their company. The Light of Jesus is that His blood alone can take away the sin that we live in. This eternal cure for our sin, that so easily oppresses us, is His blood, which cleanses; not some sin but from "every sin". This is the Truth to which John is bringing to light and that is the Light in which we must live. This Truth, light and forgiveness of sin gives to us the joy of the Lord.

"If we say that we have no sin, we deceive ourselves and the truth is not in us." **Vs. 8**

We read in **Romans 3:23** *"for all have sinned and fall short of the glory of God,"* **NKJV** and in **Romans 6:23** *"For the wages of sin is death, but the gift of God is eternal life in Christ Jesus our Lord."* **NKJV** We are born in sin and we die in sin but the believer can have forgiveness of his sin by taking Jesus as his Lord and Savior and then the blood of Jesus cleanses that sin and changes it to the righteousness of Jesus. Everyone sins and everyone has sin in his life. What is being presented here is that we are going to sin and hiding our heads in the sand to think that we have no sin is nothing but a lie and the truth is not part of us. We must understand that even when we become a follower of Christ we will still have to deal with sin. This is a world of sin and it is not heaven. Satan is the prince and power of this earth and not until Jesus returns to take us to the new heaven and the new earth will we be free from the pull of sin.

"If we confess our sins, He is faithful and just to forgive us our sins, and to cleanse us from all unrighteousness." **Vs. 9**

In that we live in a sinful world surrounded by the power of Satan and encouraged by the world to engage in sin, we will many times fall to that temptation and sin. When we do it is necessary that we admit our sin and confess those sins to God. God is just to forgive our sins because of the righteousness of His Son Jesus whose righteousness we have been covered. We can depend on the Father to forgive us for He takes our unrighteousness and exchanges it for that righteousness of His Son Jesus. **2 Corinthians 5:21**

"If we say that we have not sinned, we make Him a liar, and His word is not in us." **Vs. 10**

Sin in this world is an every day problem; Jesus said it and we must believe it. Jesus came to correct our standing before the Father and He accomplished that mission perfectly. The believer must come to the Light, believe the Truth, trust Him, obey Him and follow Him.

To add anything else is to call Him a liar, yet we are the lying one and do not want to believe the Word of Life. Jesus is Truth, Jesus is light and in Him there is no darkness at all.

Chapter 2

"My little children, these things I write to you, so that you may not sin. And if anyone sins, we have and Advocate with the Father, Jesus Christ the righteous." **Vs. 1**

This is not a refuting of what John just wrote, it is written to make it clear or to give light to what he has just written. We will sin in this world because all have sinned and fallen short. The Gnostics felt as though they were free to sin, John is saying that we are not free from sin but we should desire to live a sin free life style. He is saying that we need to desire not to sin and to do all that we can to stay away from sinning but with all our effort we will fall to sin. So, when we fail in our striving to not sin, God has provided for us an *Advocate* with the Father and the advocate is none other that His only begotten Son, Jesus. He is our "righteous" advocate, He is dependable and is the only mediator or go between that we need.

"And He Himself is the propitiation for our sins, and not for ours only but also for the whole world." **Vs. 2**

Jesus is not only our Advocate but He is the propitiation for our sin, the only righteous and loving reason for the Father to forgive us of our sins. John wrote in his gospel in **3:16** that the love of God was so great that He sent his only Son Jesus to keep us from perishing in our sin. Propitiation means that Jesus is the appeasement of God to forgive our sin; Jesus is the righteous atonement and sacrifice for our sin. Jesus was the substitute sacrifice for our sin and having made that one sacrifice, He sat down, it was finished! **John 19:20; Hebrews 10:10 – 12**

The shedding of the blood of Jesus was more than sufficient to cover the multitude of the sin of the world but His sacrifice must be personally accepted. **John 3:18** *"He who believes in Him is not condemned; but he who does not believe is condemned already, because he has not believed in the name of the only begotten Son of God."*

"Now by this we know that we know Him, if we keep His commandments. He who says, 'I know Him', and does not keep His commandments is a liar, and the truth is not in him. But whoever keeps His word, truly the love of God is perfected in Him, by this we know that we are in Him." **Vs. 3 – 5**

How does one know for sure that he is a believer? He knows this because he seeks to keep God's commandments; he wants to love others, he wants to be like Jesus; he wants to tell others about Jesus and he wants to live in the light of Jesus; he wants to be near God and to read His Word.

Reading God's Word is listening to God speak, or reading His personal letter to us; praying to God is how we personally talk with God. When we are not listening to Him and are not actively engaged in talking with Him, we are where Satan can talk with us and lead us astray and God does not want Satan near us. We must resist Satan and draw near to God, talk with God and listen to God. **James 4:7 & 8**

So, if you say that you are a believer and don't listen to God or talk with God, then you are a liar and you are living in darkness away from His glorious light. The person who is in the dark, has no idea of how things actually are. I could say that he is ignorant of what is true, this person is clueless of the situation in which he happens to be. If this is descriptive of your life, then, there is reason to doubt your salvation. If you have no "truth" in you, you are living a "lie" and if there is no "light" in you, you are living in the "dark". God is Truth, God is light and God is love. Remember this: *"This is the message which we have heard from Him and declare to you, that God is light and in Him is no darkness at all."* **1:5 NKJV**

Jesus said: *"By this all will know that you are My disciples, if you have love for one another."* **John 13:35 NKJV** As the love of God is perfected in us it becomes more and more evident that we are His disciples and we become more and more confident that we definitely are His. Loving God and loving others is what the Gospel is all about. As God has loved us we also ought to love one another. This is a description of a life for God, lived in confidence and assurance.

"He who says he abides in Him ought, himself also to walk just as He walked." **Vs. 6**

Isn't it evident that if we are living in Christ that He is in us because we are in Him? If we are in Him we must then be walking with Him. **John 15:10 NKJV** *"If you keep My commandments, you will abide in My love, just as I have kept My Father's commandments and abide in His love."*

Again, Jesus is our example; follow His example. Live as Jesus lived, walk as He walked for He is our example.

Brethren, I write no new commandment to you, but an old commandment which you have had from the beginning. The old commandment is the word which you heard from the beginning. Again, a new commandment I write to you, which thing is true in Him and in you, because the darkness is passing away, and the true light is already shining. He who says he is in the light, and hates his brother, is in darkness until now. He who loves his brother abides in the light, and there is no cause for stumbling in him. But he who hates his brother is in darkness and walks in darkness, and does not know where he is going, because the darkness has blinded his eyes." **Vs. 7 – 11**

This is not a new commandment that John is writing about but rather a new reminder of an old commandment which Jesus had taught. John wants the reader to have a clearer understanding of what that old commandment means; that commandment of loving one another, John reminds them of the foundational commandment which he told them at the start of their new faith: to love one another, the commandment of love. What is this love of God all about? This love of God does not fade but becomes brighter and brighter with each passing day in which one spends in the presence of The Light of God; it grows and becomes more and more meaningful with each passing day.

Hate and love do not coexist. Hate rejects love and love dispels hate. For someone to say he is with The Light and has hate for another is living in the shadows and is not living a life much different that the life he once lived without Christ. If we are to be known by our love for one another, where is it that hate is found? Hate can blind you, hate can overtake you and keep you from achieving all of what God has for you. What is happening is that if hate is in your life you are blindly living a lie. Hate grows, it does not fade, the love of God grows, it does not fade. Love is light and light and love overtakes darkness and hate. Take heed if you have hate in your life.

"I write to you little children, because your sins are forgiven you for His name sake. I write to you, fathers, because you have known Him who is from the beginning. I write to you, young men, because you have overcome the wicked one. I write to you, little children, because you have known the Father. I have written to you, fathers, because you have known Him who is from the beginning. I have written to you young men, because you are strong and the word of God abides in you, And you have overcome the wicked one.." **Vs. 12 - 14**

This letter is for everyone from the old to the young. We all have needs, we all have successes and we all will experience times of difficulties.

Little children have not experienced a great deal in life other than the love of their parents. In the short life of a young believer they have been comforted by the love and forgiveness of God their Father. They have witnessed Him to be a very present help and have come to trust Him in life. They have known God to be a good Father and trust Him because of His strength and character displayed in their young lives. They trust His love and do not doubt God's personal Word. They just trust God with the faith of a little child. They have come to know God's forgiveness given in response to His great love.

Forgiveness is not a wage for things they have done but a gift given because of what Jesus has done. **Romans 6:23** *"For the wages of sin is death, but the gift of God is eternal life in Christ Jesus our Lord."* Children need to understand this.

Fathers are those who have been a believer for a good time and in that time frame they have come to know that God is faithful to do what He says He will do. They know that they can trust God. Time has proven God to be all that He has said that He is and can be trusted to do all that He said He will do.

John writes to the young, strong men because of their great passion and desire of getting into the battle; using the training that they have acquired; they are using what they have learned from God's Word which is deep within them and are presently and are aggressively engaged in battle. They are fighting the good fight; they are experiencing victories.

They say that repetition is the mother of learning as so, John repeats his exhortation here to the believers.

"Do not love the world or the things in the world. If anyone loves the world, the love of the Father is not in him. For all that is in the world-the lust of the flesh, the lust of the eyes and the pride of life-is not of the Father but is of the world. And the world is passing away, and the lust of it; but he who does the will of God abides forever." **Vs. 15 – 17**

Jesus told his disciples that you cannot have two masters: *"No servant can serve two masters: for either he will hate the one, and have love for the other; or else he will hold to the one, and despise the other, You cannot sere God and man."* **Luke 16:13 NKJV** Here John warns the believer that you cannot love this world or you cannot follow the dictates of society and at the same time follow the commands of God. You cannot follow both because they oppose each other; because they are two different roads. *"There is a way that seems right to a man but its end is the way of death."* **Proverbs 14:12 NKJV** *"Your ears shall hear behind you, saying, 'This is the way, walk in it."* **Isaiah 30:21 NKJV** Jesus told His disciples *"I am the way,..."* **John 14:6 NKJV** The truth is this: God's ways are not man's ways; God's way is light and truth while man's ways are nothing but a lie and darkness.

We have a choice in all things, to love God and follow Him or to love the world, society and others. The choice is ours.

There is a process here:

1. The lust or the desire of the flesh; our natural tendency

2. The lust of eyes or our desires or cravings for what we see; our natural tendency.

3. The pride of having what the world has; which is also a natural tendency.

This happened in the Garden of Eden: Eve saw what was not hers, Eve desired what was not hers to have and Eve craved to have that which was not hers to have but reserved for God alone. Satan had put into the mind of Eve as well as Adam a desire to be like God in knowledge. She resented God keeping this knowledge from her.

191

Satan became her master, not God. **Genesis 3:6** *"So when the woman saw that the tree was good for food, that it was pleasant to the eyes, and a tree desirable to make one wise, she took of its fruit and ate, She also gave to her husband with her, and he ate."* **NKJV**

John said that this process was true then and that it remains true today and that it will always be true on this sinful earth because this is the ploy of Satan. The ways of the world are coming to an end but the way of God will last through out eternity. Satan also used it upon Jesus in the wilderness temptation but it failed there.

John assures the reader that God's way will never end, it will never fail and that His way will endure through eternity. God can be trusted.

"Little children, it is the last hour; and as you have heard that the Antichrist is coming, even now many antichrists have come, by which we know that it is the last hour." **Vs. 18**

John considered those to whom he was writing as little children, children of God and children who were placed under his protection and guidance. He cared for them with the love of Christ.

What John wanted them to understand was that danger was not something that was coming or would be coming but that it was presently upon them. They had been warned of "The Antichrist" coming in the last days and they needed to live their lives with the understanding that he was already at work during these final days before the return of Christ. Peter tells us that time means nothing to God because He is not bound by time. **2 Peter 3:8 NKJV** *"But beloved, do not forget this one thing, that with the Lord one day is as a thousand years, and a thousand years as one day."* Therefore, be diligent in your faith. They had seen many at that time who were "antichrist" they were actively working against Christ and there would be many more of these but the actual Antichrist was already working to empower those antichrists.

We must live with this expectancy as well.

"They went out from us, but they were not of us; for if they had been of us, they would have continued with us; but they went out that they might be made manifest, that none of them were of us." **Vs. 19**

These antichrist, were at one time people who were supposedly worshiping with the true believers but they soon were exposed by their false doctrine and opposition of Christ Jesus and left. They tried to carry with them all the unsuspecting as they could. As the believer looks back they can see them for what they actually were and who the are; they were not really believers in the first place, as John writes: *"none of them were of us."*

The lesson here is to test the spirits to see if they are actually of God. **1 John 4:1** *"Beloved, do not believe every spirit, but test the spirits, whether they are of God; because many false prophets have gone out into the world."* **NKJV**

"But you have an anointing from the Holy One, and you know all things." **Vs. 20**

The Holman Bible Dictionary describes an anointing as *"an outward proclamation of an appointment to office or a symbol of God's power and presence upon a person."* The believer has the power of the Holy Spirit upon him; the responsibility of the Holy Spirit to the believer is to teach, guide and empower the believer.

When a person takes Jesus Christ as their Lord and Savior, at that moment the Holy Spirit becomes present with them and upon them and He begins to teach, to lead and to empower that new believer. The Holy Spirit is also the third person of the God Head (Triune God: three in one); the Holy Spirit draws a person to God and convicts a person of their sin and of their need of a Savior. Jesus tells us that the Holy Spirit "proceeds" from the Father (**John 15:26** *"But when the Helper comes, whom I shall send to you from the Father, the Spirit of Truth who proceeds from the Father, He will testify of me."* **NKJV** Jesus sends Him and He comes from the Father. The Holy Spirit points men to Jesus and then when they take Jesus as their Savior, the Holy Spirit dwells within them to teach and empower them.

A few places where we read of the Holy Spirit are:

- **John 14 & 16** The duty of the Holy Spirit
- **2 Corinthians 1:21** We are sealed by the Holy Spirit as a guarantee of our salvation. It is God's seal of approval.
- **Ephesians 4:30 Cautioned** not to grieve the Holy Spirit or cause sorrow to the Holy Spirit by the way we live.
- **Galatians 5:22 – 26 The** Fruit of the Spirit described.

The Holy Spirit is from Jesus and the Father as a confidence and a protector against false teaching and preaching and prophecy. Luke writes in **Acts 17:28 NKJV** *"for in Him we live and move and have our being . . ."* The believer must take advantage of this power within us and rely upon the Holy Spirit as our teacher.

The Holy Spirit is our Teacher and Counselor and He leads us in the right way and in the Truth. *"However, when He, the Sprit of truth, has come, He will guide you into all truth; for He will not speak on His own authority, but whatever He hears He will speak and He will tell you things to come."* **John 16:13 NKJV**

If the Holy Spirit is in us then the Truth is in us and we have confidence that He will guide us in all things.

"I have not written to you because you do not know the truth, but because you know it, and that no lie is of the truth. Who is a liar but he who denies that Jesus is the Christ? He is antichrist who denies the Father and the Son. Whoever denies the Son does not have the Father either; he who acknowledges the Son has the Father also," **Vs. 21 – 23**

Jesus told His disciples that if they had seen Him then they have seen the Father because He and the Father were one. **John 14:10** *"Do you not believe that I am in the Father, and the Father is Me? The words that I speak to you I do not speak on My own authority; but the Father who dwells in Me doe the works."* **NKJV**

They knew this but they needed to be warned not to accept everyone out of kindness. They must feel an obligation for Truth and reject any hint of contradiction to the Truth. The Truth is either all true or it is a lie. There is no shadow in the light of the Truth. Any teaching that is in any way slanted from the Truth is to be considered a lie and a lie of the Devil.

The truth is Jesus and the Father; the person who acknowledges the majesty and praiseworthiness of Jesus and the Father is of God all others are lies of the Devil.

"Therefore, let that abide in you which you heard from the beginning. If what you heard from the beginning abides in you, you also will abide in the Son and the Father, And this is the promise that He has promised us-eternal life." **Vs. 24 & 25**

The Gospel of Christ does not change because God does not change. We are to question anyone who claims to have a new word from the Lord or something other than what is already written in Scripture. Scripture is complete, it is to be understood as it is written.

My Dad, Glenn Thomas, had the following statement written in the front of one of his study Bibles and it is something that will always be true. I do not know how he came upon it; I am not sure if he read it somewhere, heard some say it or if it is thought of his own and from his personal study but these are the words written:

"The task of the scholar is to guarantee the purity of the text, to get as close as possible to the Word as originally given. He may compare Scripture with Scripture until he discovers the true meaning of the text. But right there his authority ends. He must never sit in judgment upon what is written. He must not bring the meaning of the Word before the bar of his reason."

Error begins with someone giving an opinion, the opinion is only as trustworthy as the person giving it. Opinion is not fact, opinion is what one person thinks within his limited knowledge and understanding. Limited knowledge give place to error and I would rather trust an "All knowing being". How about you?

"These things I have written to you concerning those who try to deceive you. But the anointing which you have received from Him abides in you, and you do not need that anyone teach you; but as the same anointing teaches you concerning all things, and is true, and is not a lie, and just as it has taught you, you will abide in Him." **Vs. 26 & 27**

It is the aim of false teachers to deceive. The word "false" says it all; they teach false things, or lies and do not have the Truth to be able to teach. The Truth is unknown to them and all they know is a lie. They are a deceiver of The Deceiver. **2 John 7** *For many deceivers have gone out into the world who do not confess Jesus Christ as coming in the flesh. This is a deceiver and an antichrist."* **NKJV; John 10:10** *"The thief does not come except to steal, and to kill and to destroy. I have come that they may have life, and that they may have it more abundantly."* **NKJV**

Again, the Holy Spirit lives within us and is in us as a Teacher and gives us guidance in any situation. Use the Holy Spirit.

"And now, little children, abide in Him that when He appears, we may have confidence and not be ashamed before him at His coming. If you know that He is righteous, you know that everyone who practices righteousness is born of Him." **Vs. 27 & 28**

Our drive in life ought to be that we would not do anything to be ashamed of at the return of Jesus. If we live righteously and seek to become more and more like our righteous Lord then we will be anxious for His return and we will be confident as we stand before Him.

A righteous God cannot send an unrighteous messenger. Any messenger, teacher or leader from God lives in righteousness, teaches righteousness and seeks to live more righteously. The righteous person desires to glorify His Righteous Lord and Savior Jesus Christ because he has His righteousness upon him. This person does not want to do anything in his life that would dishonor his God. This type of person can be trusted and this person's sprit bears witness with our spirit. There is a brotherhood that is felt between believers.

Chapter 3

"Behold what manner of love the Father has bestowed upon us that we should be called children of God! Therefore the world does not know us, because it did not know Him." **Vs. 1**

"Children of God"! Wow! How can this be? Why would God do this? What kind of love does it take for a Holy God to call us His children? I do not understand this. We don't deserve it by any stretch of the imagination. Who can describe that feeling? God "bestowed" it upon us, He has allowed us to be called "children of God". The angels marvel at this. Satan can't stand it but Jesus loves it and the Father enjoys it. Jesus said: *"Let the little children come to Me, and do not forbid them; for of such is the kingdom of heaven."* **Matthew 19:14 NKJV**

The world doesn't know us, the world does not understand us and hates us; because they did not know nor did they understand Jesus but they hated Jesus. Why should we expect anything different? The important thing is the eternal thing; that is to be loved, endeared, desired and understood by God.

"Beloved, now we are children of God and it has not yet been revealed what we shall be, but we know that when He is revealed, we shall be like Him, for we shall see Him as He is. And everyone who has this hope in Him purifies himself, just at He is pure." **Vs. 2 & 3**

Again, John goes to the thought of the believer being a child of God. He says yes, it is hard to believe but it is true and it is also true that we will live for eternity as God's adopted children in God's new heaven and earth.

What heaven is like we can not know exactly other than what we read in Scripture. We can take confidence in what we do know about Jesus and what He is like. Then we do know we will be like Him! That is enough! All other ideas of heaven are just that – ideas. Ideas are alright but they are not Scripture. We have our ideas and we ought not to get upset and agitated with the ideas of other believer's ideas and perceptions of heaven that do not line up with ours. We can, however, be excited about being with Jesus.

Lanny Wolfe wrote the song <u>Jesus Will Be What Makes it Heaven for Me</u> that he published in 1972 with these lyrics:

> *I've heard of a land that is wondrously fair,*
> *God's Word says it's splendor is far beyond compare;*
> *In the place that's called heaven my soul wants to be,*
> *For where Jesus is will be heaven for me.*
>
> *Heaven for me, heaven for me,.*
> *Jesus will be what makes it heaven for me.*
> *All it's beauty and wonders I'm longing to see,*
> *But Jesus will be what makes it heaven for me.*

I love these lyrics for they reflect my idea of heaven. Although I lack much understanding and knowledge about heaven; I do know that Jesus will be there and I do know that our whole existence for being there is for the glory of God and because of the work of Jesus. I do know that we will be like Jesus, I do know that I will be there as an adopted son of God. With that little understanding, I can joy and take comfort.

Jesus is our hope, our assurance and with these thoughts of heaven the believer can be impassioned to purify his life to live more and more like Jesus here on this earth as His ambassador. The believer can strive to be holy as He is holy.

Whoever commits sin also commits lawlessness, and sin is lawlessness and you know that he was manifested to take away our sins, and in Him there is no sin. Whoever abides in Him does not sin. Whoever sins has neither seen Him nor known Him. Little children, let no one deceive you. He who practices righteousness is righteous just as He is righteous. He who sins is of the devil, for the devil has sinned form the beginning. For this purpose, the Son of God was manifested, that he might destroy the works of the devil. Whoever has been born of God does not sin, for His seed remains in him; and he cannot sin, because he has been born of God." **Vs. 4 – 9**

Sin is what Jesus came to do away with. God cannot even look upon sin because He is holy and has holy eyes. The punishment for sin is death but God is not willing that anyone should perish but that all should come to the point of repentance of sin. **2 Peter 3:9; John 3:16 – 19**

Paul talks of the battle that we, as believers, fight everyday. **Romans 7:13 – 25** The believer lives in a constant battle but the battle is not with people it is with the spiritual world, a spiritual battle of principalities and powers in heavenly places. **Ephesians 6:12** *"For we do* *not wrestle against flesh and blood, but against principalities, against powers, against the rulers of the darkness of this age, against spiritual hosts of wickedness in the heavenly places."* **NKJV**

It is the spirit against the flesh and the flesh against the spirit each desiring to gain control. These cannot co-exist they are contrary against each other and because of this battle we cannot do the things that we wish to do. Each one has it's own way, they go down different streets, which will you choose? The battle is great but the conclusion is sure for the believer, in that, we do not do battle alone, we stand in the might and power of the Holy Spirit. **Galatians 5:16 – 18**

With this understanding of Scripture from Scripture we can look at what John writes. He is saying that the believer is in Christ and being in Christ and having His righteousness upon him we have no sin because of the righteousness of Jesus because Jesus is pure, though we are not. But while we are on this earth we will continue to be bombarded with the pull of sin and we must decide daily to whom we will yield.

Sin is not of God, it is not God Who tempts you to sin, it is the power of Satan. Sin is a falling short of the glory of God and His holiness, we read in **Romans 3:23.** The "Seed" of God is Jesus Christ His Son, His heir and in Whom there is no sin at all. **2 Corinthians 5:21** Being in Christ then we have no sin because of having our sin put upon Jesus and we are made pure by the righteousness of Jesus. Now this is all God's doing, it is all His plan and we receive it by repenting of our sin to God. This is the whole reason Jesus was "manifested" or made known to the world; for salvation from sin; this whole plan is a God thing all together and we have no part in the plan other than to repent and accept God's plan. We can do nothing to make ourselves worthy of forgiveness, Jesus is the only worthy one. We must, however, repent of our sin and strive to keep from sinning daily. When we ask forgiveness, then, God is faithful and just to forgive us of our sin. **1 John 1:9** In **1 John 2:7 & 8** John writes: *"Little children, let no one deceive you, he who 'practices righteousness' is righteous, just as He is righteous, He who sins (practices sin) is of the devil, for the devil has sinned from the beginning, for this purpose the Son of God was manifested (has come to be made known) that He might destroy the works of the devil.* **NKJV**

Now, if you are in Christ, you are in His righteous life which is sinless. Jesus is God's Seed, Jesus is God's only begotten Son and if we are in Christ then we no longer are under the punishment of sin, which is death, but we will receive New life in Christ Jesus.

Sin is always wrong, sin always falls short of God's glory and is NEVER acceptable or overlooked by God. God's desire for us is that we do not sin but when we sin we have and advocate and the advocate is Jesus Christ.

"In this the children of God and the children of the devil are manifest: Whoever does not practice righteousness is not of God, nor is he who does not love his brother. For this is the message that you heard from the beginning, that we should love one another, not as Cain who was of the wicked one and murdered, his brother. And why did he murder him? Because his works were evil and his brother's righteous. Do not marvel my brethren, if the world hates you. We know that we have passed from death to life,

because we love the brethren. He who does not love his brother abides in death. Whoever hates his brother is a murderer, and you know that no murderer has eternal life abiding in him." **Vs. 10 – 15**

The only way to love as God loves is to have the righteousness of God upon us. God is love **1 John 4:7** and God is light **1 John 1:5**. In order to see other as God sees them we must look through His eyes of love and in the light of His glory. If we do not have His righteousness upon us we cannot love as He love. If we do not have His love we have the evil eyes of Satan who is a murderer, a lier and an accuser of the brethren. If you hate your brother you are a murdered **John 8:44; Revelation 12:10**

Have you ever noticed that when a believer tries to do good in this world, it is often slandered as being done with selfish desires by the world? Why is this true? It is because the world hates Jesus and because we are His followers, they hate us. Cain hated Able because of Able's desire to worship God as God asked. Believers will always be hated by the world because Satan is their master.

The distinguishing factor of a believer is his love. Love is important and if you do not have love for others, then your love for God and your place as a child of God is in question. By this shall all men know that you are my disciple, Jesus said, if you have love one for another. **John 13:35**

"By this we know love, because He laid down His life for us. And we also ought to lay down our lives for the brethren." **Vs. 16**

John 3:16 says that God loved mankind so much that He gave his own life so that others might have life eternal. If Jesus did this and He is our example to follow, then we ought to be willing to lay down our earthly lives for the brethren. The reason we know love is because God first loved us. **1 John 4:10**

"But whoever has this world's goods, and sees his brother in need, and shuts up his heart from him, how does the love of God abide in him? My little children, let us not love in word or in tongue, but in deed and in truth." **Vs. 17 & 18**

If God gives you something, or if you have been blessed with worldly riches those riches were not given to you to build barns and banks, they were given to you to be a blessing to someone else. John tells the reader that if you see someone who has a need and you can meet that need, give what you have been given and God will be glorified. If you don't have this understanding the question is: How can you call yourself a child of the good and kind God? Don't just be a voice, be a hand. Words mean little unless the are backed by deeds. What we need to do is to determine that we want to make a difference in this world. Actions show or display Christ to others they make him "manifest" to others.

"And by this we know that we are of the truth, and shall assure our hearts before Him. For if our heart condemns us, God is greater than our heart, and knows all things. Beloved if our heart does not condemn us, we have confidence before God. And whatever we ask we receive from Him, because we keep His commandments and do those things that are pleasing in his sight. And this is the

commandment: that we should believe on the name of His Son Jesus Christ and love one another, as He gave us commandment." **Vs. 19 – 23**

If we are a person of deeds, then as we stand before God we can stand in confidence because we have been active for God. Our hearts may condemn us by making us feel, we could have done more but God is greater in understanding and He knows all things well. God knows us perfectly and the greatest thing is God and doing what He has called us to do. The question is, have we obeyed?

The commandment is two folds:

1. Believe God and His Son Jesus Christ.
2. Obey God and His Son Jesus Christ by loving other. And Share the Gospel with all.

"Now he who keeps His commandments abides in Him, and He in him. And by this we know that He abides in us."

A life of close fellowship with God is a life that has been spent in close conversation with God, reading His Word, Speaking to Him in prayer, personal prayer. The Holy Spirit that Jesus left with us abides in us and is our assurance and guarantee of God's power in us and that we are definitely children of the Father.

Chapter 4

"Beloved, do not believe every spirit, but test the spirits, whether they are of God; because many false prophets have gone out into the world. By this you know the Spirit of God: Every spirit that confesses that Jesus Christ has come in the flesh is of God, and every spirit that does not confess that Jesus Christ has come in the flesh is not of God. And this is the spirit of the Antichrist, which you have heard was coming, and is now already in the world." **Vs. 1 - 3**

Just because someone is a preacher or a teacher does not give them credibility as a proclaimer of the Truth. Question them, feel an obligation to challenge them and test them. A false teacher is not a rarity in this world, a false teacher is a common thing and they are to be expected. They are from Satan and they spread the spirit and message of Antichrist. They are all around us today.

The test is this: Do they believe that Jesus Christ is the only begotten Son of God Who was sent to this world, born of a virgin to be the sacrifice for the sin of the world? Do they believe that He actually died and actually rose again from the grave, ascended to heaven and will be coming back again? The Gnostics of the early church did not believe this and there are still those today who deny this.

"You are of God, little children, and have overcome them, because He who is in you is greater than he who is in

the world. They are of the world. Therefore, they speak as of the world, and the world hears them. We are of God. He who knows God hears us; he who is not of God does not hear us. But this we know the spirit of truth and the spirit of error." **Vs. 4 – 6**

As the believer lives in this world he faces challenges that takes issue to his faith. We have these challenges and battles because we are in the world and Satan controls this world. The believer then must expect challenges and battles all the while having this understanding: *God has overcome the world by the work of His Son Jesus Christ.* With that understanding and the added knowledge that the believer is a child of God, we then as His heirs, benefit from His conquest and we through Him are overcomers and conquerors. **Romans 8:37**

Do not allow the rhetoric and propaganda of the world cause us to take our eyes of our Father. We have conquered by the blood of Jesus (**Revelation 1:5; Colossians 1:11 – 14; 1 John 5:4**) Yes we have overcome but the false teachers, prophets and preachers of the lie are active and will not let up in their relentless push to slander The Truth of God. The key to living joyfully in this battle is the understanding: God's Word is The Truth and it will stand true in every battle and it is His Word that exposes the lie of the world and those who proclaim the error.

"Beloved, let us love one another, for love is of God; and everyone who loves is born of God and knows God. He who does not love does not know God for God is love." **Vs. 7 & 8**

The epistle of **1 John** is filled with expositions of the love of God. Here we read: *"Beloved"* and in **Ephesians 1:6** Paul writes of the Father making us acceptable in *"the beloved"*, Jesus is the beloved Son of God. Here in **verse 7** John calls the reader, beloved, and being beloved we need to love one another just because we are acceptable in "The Beloved" and being in Him Who is love we ought to love others as well. If you are born of God who is love and we have come to know Him then, naturally, we ought to love others. The shocking check and balance here is if you do not love, you have great reason to wonder about your salvation in Christ Jesus. If you do not love others, how can you say that you know and love God? Because God is love!

"In this the love of God was manifested toward us, that God sent His only begotten Son into the world, that we might live through Him. In this love, not that we loved God, but that he loved us and sent His Son to be the propitiation for our sins. Beloved, if God so loved us, we also ought to love one another." **Vs. 9 - 11**

The love of God was first expressed to the world by the sending of His Only Begotten Son to the World to do the acceptable and required work needed for God to be able to forgive sin. The only way was God's way and there is no other way, there is no other person that could do this work. *"Nor is there salvation in any other, for there is no other name under heaven given among men by which we must be saved,"* **Acts 4:12 NKJV**

"For He made Him who knew no sin to be sin for us, that we might become the righteousness of God in Him." **2 Corinthians 5:21 NKJV**

The reason we love God is because He first expressed His love to us and because of His first act of love we love Him. It is also true that because of His first act of love we also ought to love others first and not love in response to their loving us first.

"No one has seen God at any time. If we love one another, God abides in us, and His love has been perfected in us. By this we know that we abide in Him, and He in us, because He have given us of His Spirit. And we have seen and testify that the Father has sent the Son as Savior of the world. Whoever confesses that Jesus is the Son of God, God abides in him and he in God. And we have known and believed the love that God has for us. God is love and he who abides in love abides in God, and God in him." **Vs. 12 – 16**

The bottom line is God is True Love and if you live in God and God lives in you then you have the love of God flowing through you. If that love is truly in you then you will have the ability to see others as God sees them and you will have the loving desire of God to express His love to others in the genuine love of God. As we express His love the mere expression of that love gives us the assurance that we are of God and are His children.

The Epistle of **1 John** is filled with the "love of God" and if this epistle is so saturated with it then this love of God must be of supreme importance to the life of the believer. We live and take our being in His love and it is in His love that we can cast out the fear of life. **Vs. 18**

The believer needs to love God and love others, not because we have to but because we want to in order to be more and more like God. Don't love people because of what they have done for you but love them so they will know that we are followers of Christ Jesus.

"Love has been perfected among us in this: that we may have boldness in the Day of Judgment; because as He is, so are we in this world. There is no fear in love; but perfect love casts out fear, because fear involves torment. But he who fears has not been made perfect in love. We love Him because He first loved us." **Vs. 17– 19**

What is perfect love? Perfect love is having confidents in the lover or the one expressing love and promising lasting love. God is not only perfect love but He is pure Truth and you can trust what he says. If God loves us, then you can depend upon His love toward us. Perfect love has no cause for fear and mistrust of the Lover, perfect love cast out all fear. The only reason one might question God's love is a thought that Satan might bring to us. Say: Get thee behind me Satan.

If someone says, 'I love God', and hates his brother, he is a liar; for he who does not love his brother whom he has seen, how can he love God whom he has not seen? And this is the commandment we have from Him: that he who love God must love his brother." **Vs. 20 & 21**

Just because you say you love God does not mean that you know God. A cause for someone to question his position in God would be if he has hate for a brother or someone. Hate is not of God hate is of the Devil. Love is of God because God is love. If you say that you love God and are one of His children, then you must have love for one another. Jesus commanded it and love is the icon of Christ.

Chapter 5

"Whoever believes that Jesus is the Christ is born of God, and everyone who love Him who begot also loves him who is begotten of Him. By this we know that we love the children of God, when we love God and keep His commandments. For this is the love of God, that we keep His commandments, and His commandments are not burdensome. **Vs. 1 - 3**

How does a believer know for certain that he is an actual believer and follower of God or a true child of God?

- Do you really believe that Jesus is the promised Messiah and sent from the Father?
- Do you love God the Father?
- Do you love other believers and want to be around them with them?
- Do you love to "<u>obey</u>" the commandments of God?

If God is love and you have the love of God displayed in your life and you love to obey Gods' commandments; you strive to do those things that He commands and it is a joy, not a burden to you in doing them then, you are a true believer.

To believe that Jesus is the Son of God is to love as Jesus asked us to love. God does not hate people; He hates sin. Loving others is not a burden upon the believer; it is a blessing to love others as Jesus loved us. It is by loving others that we can point others to God. As they see His goodness and love demonstrated in our actions they see God. In **Romans 4:8** we read: *"But God demonstrated His own love toward us, in that while we were still sinners, Christ died for us," "Or do you despise the riches of His goodness, forbearance and longsuffering, not knowing that the goodness of God leads you to repentance?"* **Romans 2:4 NKJV**

To love others and do good to others is a sure way to point others to Christ; to show them Christ.

"For what ever is born of God overcomes the world. And this is t he victory that has overcome the world – our faith. Who is he who overcomes the world, but he who believes that Jesus is the Son of God." **Vs. 4 & 5**

God has already overcome the world by His powerful work which was done through His Son Jesus believer is a sojourner here in this world until He returns. As we sojourn we experience the battle with the evil of this world. God's love gives us the power to overcome the pull of the world and to endure the attacks of Satan. Faith, the shield of faith (**Ephesians 6:16**) is our defense in standing for God in the battle. We cannot win without our shield of faith.

We may indeed die upon this earth but we will for certain live forever in that special place that He has prepared for us. It is appointed for all people to die once but we don't have to die twice or we don't have to die physically and spiritually. As we live upon this earth, live in the expectancy of Christ's return and not upon the ever-present difficulties and sufferings that we must also endure upon this earth. They are temporary and they are passing away.

If a person does not believe that Jesus is who He says He is with confident faith, then we cannot expect to live a successful and happy life in Christ Jesus on this earth. A life without faith is a fearful life and fear does not come from God but our adversary the Devil. The believers love for others strengthens his belief and faith in Christ and will create confidence in life, and an assurance of a <u>sure</u> victory in the work of Christ Jesus. If you want to win then you must not doubt; doubt weakens one while confidence and faith encourages one with added power.

Paul writes these things in **2 Corinthians 4:16 – 18 NKJV**

"Therefore, we do not lose heart. Even though our outward man is perishing, yet the inward man is being renewed day by day. For our light affliction, which is but for a moment, is working for us a far more exceeding and eternal weight of glory, while we do not look at the things which are seen, but the things which are not seen. For the things which are seen are temporary, but the things which are not seen are eternal."

Being children of God's love we must not lose heart in our mission. The believer must always remember that this world, in which we live, is a short one. This world and the things of this world will one day perish and in place of this "temporary" world we will inherit an eternal new earth and new heaven from God.

Our struggle in life is, after all, bound in the context of time and time will end one day. We grow old, we suffer and we do get discouraged but all of this is merely temporary, it will be gone one day. The reward for our endurance is the Kingdom of God and being able to experience His eternal glory. We can only think of these things now and those thoughts are so much greater than our ability to understand today but we will understand one day for we shall see it all. The things that God has for us is beyond description or of our ability to think or dream. The things of eternity are God things, God thoughts and exceeding and abundantly above us. These things cannot be seen now but they can be joyfully expected. With this great hope keep your eyes and mind upon them and off the things of this visible earth.

"This is He who came by water and blood-Jesus Christ; not only by water, but by water and blood. And it is the Spirit who bears witness, because the Spirit is truth. For there are three that bear witness in heaven: the Father, the Word, and the Holy Spirit: and these three are one. And there are three that bear witness on earth: the Spirit the water, and the blood, and these three agree as one." **Vs. 6 – 8**

Jesus is the one who came and was validated and confirmed in Heaven as God's Son by the very voice of the Father in the transfiguration recorded in **Matthew 17:5** and the Holy Spirit at the baptism of Jesus by John the Baptist, recorded in **John 1:32 – 34** and by Jesus, the Word. These three: the Father, the Son and the Holy Spirit validate Jesus. They are the Trinity or the Triune God. These are The Truth.

There is also three witnesses of the truth of Jesus as the Messiah on earth and they are by the baptism by water of Jesus; the miracles and deeds of Jesus, the death on the cross and resurrection of Jesus from the grave. The disciples and men saw these things as they happened and they are also witnesses. These are a truth.

"If we receive the witness of men, the witness of God is greater, for this is the witness of God which He has testified of His Son. He who believes in the Son of God has the witness in himself, he who does not believe God has made Him a liar, because he has not believed in the testimony that God has given of His Son. And this is the testimony: that God has given us eternal life, and this life is in His Son. He who has the Son has life; he who does not have the Son of God does not have life. These things I have written to you who believe in the name of the Son of God, that you may know that you have eternal life and that you may continue to believe in the name of the Son of God." **Vs. 9 – 13**

How good of the life one lives is not the measure for entrance into God's heaven and the gift of eternal life. The measure is belief, trust, acceptance and obedience of God's Word. If a person lives a so-called model life and rejects the gift of God's Son, they are calling God's Son a liar and His gift as unnecessary. If a person rejects this free gift and only acceptable sacrifice, then God will reject that person; depart from me, I never knew you. *"Then He will also say to those on the left hand, 'Depart from Me, you cursed, into the everlasting fire prepared of the devil and his angels.. . .and these will go away into everlasting punishment, but the righteous into eternal life."* **Matthew 25:41 & 46 NKJV**

God is The Truth, Who has done these great things for mankind. God is telling us that He has a free gift of eternal life that is available for our taking by our just believing what He says without doubt. His "only" reason for giving us eternal life is only because of His Only Begotten Son, Jesus the Christ. It is all His work and none of our work all He asks is that we believe Him. The non-believer is calling God's Word a lie.

Simply put: if you have Jesus as Savior you have eternal life – if you don't then you keep your eternal death. John says that his reason of writing this letter is that the reader would believe God and not question Him but question anything else. John wants the believer to be sure of their salvation and continue to live a happy and confident life in Christ Jesus.

"Now this is the confidence that we have in Him, that if we ask anything according to His will, He hears us. And if we know that He hears us, whatever we ask, we know that we have the petitions that we have asked of Him." **Vs. 14 & 15**

God answers the prayer of the believer, period. This verse does not say God might hear or that it is possible for God to hear but that God hears the prayer of the believer. Now John has just established that a believer is one who loves God and obeys His commandments and the believer is one who loves others as God does for God is love. The believer lives a life totally focused on God and lived for God. With this understanding of the believer and the one asking something of God we know for certain that what is being asked is in the will of God and to be used in doing the will of God. This verse is not a "name it, claim it" verse; it is a ask and it shall be given unto you type of verse. What the true and active follower of Christ asks for, God hears and will give to him that which he has asked because it is in the will of God. If we know He hears then we can know that we will receive.

"If anyone sees his brother sinning a sin which does not lead to death, he will ask, and He will give him life for those who commit sin not leading to death. There is a sin leading to death. I do not say that he should pray about that. All unrighteousness is sin and there is sin not leading to death." **Vs. 16 & 17**

Believers live with each other and for each other in the spreading of the Good News. Everyone needs to have someone watching their back. There are many times in the life of the believer that we are under attack by the forces of the evil one and we may not be aware of the attack and we also may be in the process of losing a battle. When we see, another believer sinning a sin, that is not a sin that does not lead to death or a sin that would cause them to die, then we need to pray for that believer and God will give that believer a refreshed life. All of us need refreshing from time to time. All of us need to be around fellow believers to help us in our ministry together. If we pray for those believers then God will give them that needed forgiveness and refreshed life that they are in need.

Anything that is not good and right in the eyes of God is sin, all unrighteousness is sin for it falls short of the glory of God. There are sins, such as flagrant and willful sins even apostasy that will bring death and for those types of sin death is the only result.

"We know that whoever is born of God does not sin, but he who has been born of God keeps himself and the wicked one does not touch him. We know that we are of God, and the whole world lives under the sway of the wicked one. And we know that the Son of God has come and has given us an understanding that we may know him who is true; and we are in Him who is true, in His Son Jesus Christ. This is the true God and eternal life. Little Children, Keep yourselves from idols. Amen." **Vs. 18 – 21**

A person who is born of God has the Seed of God within him. (**3:9**) The believer does not lead a life where he practices unrighteousness or sin.   We are new creations and as a new creation; we have the Spirit of God in our lives and we live with that Seed of the Spirit of God in a fleshly or worldly body. The Spirit of God and the flesh battle daily and many times we fail not because of the Spirit in us but because of the fleshly body which we must sojourn in this world. The battle is great but the person who has the Spirit practices to be a holy person. When the pull of Satan, the principalities and powers of this world reek havoc in our lives, our faith kicks in. Satan cannot win this battle because God has already won it but Satan can cause great grief, aharm and can bring great discouragement. We can at times even begin to become overcome with our doing good. During these time, pray, lift up each other.

Remember what we have been taught in these times of discouragement and trial. As the believer experiences these times of trial, remember God is faithful and ever-present. In these times make sure that you do not turn to alternative helps thinking that they will solve the situation.

They will not solve the problem they will increase the problem; they are false idols, false teachers, false preachers and lies of the devil.

As it is written, so shall it be!

Just the Basics

Discovering the Truth in an Untruthful World

II JOHN

Introduction

The second epistle or letter of John is addressed to the *"elect lady"* or church perhaps that he had pastured. The church is the chosen body of believers that exists to equip believers; or train them for the proclamation of the Gospel. It is a support group to encourage each other and to love one another as John expresses so frequently in this epistle.

The church was under attack by false doctrine taught by false teachers and false prophets who were teaching and preaching another gospel. They denied the divinity of Christ Jesus and they were known as Gnostic preacher preaching the Gnostic Gospel. Still today we have that same false doctrine being propagated by false teachers and preachers. Therefore, the danger still remains a viable one to the church and it's body of believers.

The believer needs to understand and recognize Truth and if he recognizes Truth, lies will be evident. This epistle is short because John is planning to come to them personally which also gives reason to see the urgency of addressing this problem. John had already written of this work of the Antichrist but the error still remained.

The error was causing the church or "elect lady" to begin to see divisions within the church and the church was becoming polarized into groups with each group distrusting and despising the other. The problem was they were neglecting the love that Jesus commanded them to have for each other.

In order to remain focused on the main thing they needed to focus on the love of God for each other and recognize the error for what it was. Once they recognized the Truth and began to focus on it, then error becomes evident.

The Letter

"To the elect lady and her children, whom I love in truth, and not only I, but also, all those who have know the truth, because of the truth which abides in us and will be with us forever:" **Vs. 1 & 2**

The elect lady is the chosen body of believers of which most likely John had been or even still was the pastor. John loved them with the love of Christ as did many others who had the privilege of knowing them. They had been known as a loving church and a church of "The Truth".

Truth never changes because truth is a fact. Truth cannot be legitimately challenged because a challenge in the truth makes it something other than the truth, it is a lie. Truth abides forever. **1 Peter 1:25**

"Grace, mercy and peace will be with you from God the Father and from the Lord Jesus Christ, the Son of the Father, in truth and love." **Vs. 3**

The Gnostics did not believe that Jesus was truly God but that he became God. John links Jesus with the Father right at the beginning of his epistle. Jesus was God and He always was God and He will always be God. That is the Truth and nothing but the Truth.

John prefaces the Truth with the qualities of Truth; first Grace, which is unmerited favor, then,

Mercy which is unmerited forgiveness and finally with peace which is God's peace that is a lasting peace; it comes from God and is a peace that is indescribable in human terms. **John 14:6** *"Peace I leave with you, My peace I give to you; not as the world gives do I give to you, Let not your heart be troubles, neither let it be afraid."* **NKJV; Philippians 4:7** *"And the peace of God, which surpasses all understanding, will guard your hearts and minds through Christ Jesus."* **NKJV**

"I rejoiced greatly that I have found some of your children walking in the truth, as we received commandment from the Father, and now I plead with you, lady, not as though I wrote a new commandment to you, but that which we have had from the beginning: that we love one another." **Vs. 4 & 5**

John's joy is that "some" of the believers were walking in the truth which means that many were not walking in the Truth. Paul reproves the Galatians' church for many of them being led away "so soon". *"I marvel that you are turning away so soon from Him who called you in the grace of Christ, to a different gospel, which is not another; but there are some who trouble you and want to pervert the gospel of Christ. But even if we, or an angel from heave preach any other gospel to you than what we have preached to you, let him be accursed."* **Galatians 1:6 – 9 NKJV**

The Truth does not need to be revised in any way; Truth is truth and the church needs to get a grasp of this fact. Some other gospel is a false

228

gospel and that is what was being preached to this *"elect lady"* or body of believers. The problem was wide spread but John was protecting his flock.

"This is love, that we walk according to His commandments. This is the commandment, that as you have heard from the beginning, you should walk in it." **Vs. 6**

If you are not walking or living your life in love, then you must be living your life in a lie. If you live in a lie then the Truth is not with you and you are living a lie and spreading a lie unwittingly. You may be sincere, or perhaps have good intentions but with all your good intentions and sincerity you are sincerely wrong.

The way you are going and the information that you have may seem to be right but the truth is, you are going in the wrong direction, with wrong information and it will result or end in an unintended conclusion; it leads to death. **Proverbs 14:12** *"There is a way that seems right to a man, but its end is the way of death."* **NKJV**

The Holy Spirit is our guide and when we are trusting in Him as our teacher and guide, then if we take a wrong way, we will hear behind us the gentle voice of our Teacher: **Isaiah 30:21** *"Your ears shall hear a word behind you, saying, 'This is the way, walk in it"* **NKJV** This is nothing new, this has been taught from the beginning and we need to know and be reminded of the Truth.

"For many deceivers have gone out into the world who do not confess Jesus Christ as coming in flesh. This is a deceiver and an antichrist." **Vs. 7**

The deceivers were the Gnostics who did not believe that God, Who is a Spirit and good; could live in human flesh, which they defined as material and evil. These false teachers could not understand because they gave credibility to human understanding of the day and held it in greater regard or trusted it above spiritual understanding. Therefore, spiritual truth gave way to human thought; Scripture did not matter to them and they believed a lie.

The Truth is that The Father sent His Only Begotten Son into a wicked world of evil to cleanse them of their evil and sin. The only way was God's Son, Jesus and that is a fact, it is truth and there is no additional truth to be added to this.

These false teachers were being used by the Deceiver, Satan, and they were also the works of antichrist.

"Look to yourselves that we do not lose those things we worked for, but that we may receive a full reward. Whoever transgresses and does not abide in the doctrine of Christ does not have God. He who abides in the doctrine of Christ has both the Father and the Son. If anyone comes to you and does not bring this doctrine, do not receive him into your house nor greet him; for he who greets him shares in his evil deeds." **Vs. 8 - 11**

The warning was true then and is even truer today. Don't mess up your life in Christ by being tainted by the error of false teachers, you will be losing many rewards which you have worked for so hard. If we take time to listen to error we will soon be tainted by that error and may even become part of spreading the lie that they teach. Don't let them into your house, don't listen to these false teachers! Flee these people and make their evil intentions known to other believers. They are evil and all their deeds are evil as well. They may have a warm and glowing personality; Yes, they may be likable but their works are of the devil who comes to us as an angel of light.

"Having many things to write to you, I did not wish to do so with paper and ink; but I hope to come to you and speak face to face, that our joy may be full. The children of your elect sister greet you. Amen." **Vs. 12 & 13**

John closes the letter by informing them that he plans to come to them personally and he was most likely living in Ephesus at the time. With that understanding John was acknowledging that the believers at the church where he was writing this epistle were praying for this body of believers as they battled the onslaught of the devil. John wanted to deal with this problem personally and felt that it was so dire that it required his personal presence.

With this John closes this brief letter with the word: *"Amen"* As it is written so shall it be.

Just the Basics

Discovering the Truth in an Untruthful World

III John

Introduction

The greatest problem people have in life is the struggle for power, success and gaining a victory over difficulties that we experience in life. The power struggle is not limited to things of life only but it is very evident within the walls of the church.

The problem with believers is that we are not supposed to be masters but slaves and servants of Christ Jesus and working together for the cause of Christ and not to give precedence of our own goals to the goals of Christ's Gospel.

The main thing here is the main thing of the other epistle of John which is The Truth and The Commandment of love given to us by Jesus. The trouble maker here is Diotrephes who struggled to gain preeminence and the good example believer in the church which was Demetrius. It is Jesus Who has the preeminence in the Church and in our lives not any other thing.

The Letter

"The elder, to the beloved Gaius, who I love in truth:"

The elder is John and Gaius is the recipient of the epistle. There is not a clear understanding as to which Gaius this pastor actually was only that he was beloved and that he loved The Truth. Gaius was a common name of the day and there is no certainty of his identity other than pastor here. It is not evident that this Gaius is the same person that is mentioned by Paul or others. **Romans 16:23**

The problem at the church was that of false teachers. False teacher still plague the true church today. False teachers seek recognition, money and fame, they pray on the unsuspecting, the weak and untrained.

Here John recognizes Gaius, the pastor, and thereby, gives him credibility as a true, quality and trustworthy minister of the Gospel of Jesus Christ. Gaius is not seeking preeminence, but Jude gives to him preeminence as one that the church can be trust to teach Truth.

The church knew Gaius but we do not, the mere fact that we do not know who Gaius is, speaks volumes to the reader, as to what is prestigious in the eyes of God. Gaius was successful for doing what God called him to do, success does not mean that others recognize you but that

God does. God recognizes the obedient to His Word. The disciples struggled with recognition and position and Jesus dealt with them often. *"What was it you disputed among yourselves on the road? But they kept silent, for on the road they had disputed among themselves who would be the greatest. And He sat down, called the twelve, and said to them, 'If anyone desires to be first, he shall be last of all and servant of all."* **Mark 9:33 – 35 NKJV**

John understood this pull for preeminence and he would deal with it as well.

"Beloved, I pray that you may prosper in all things and be in health, just as your soul prospers. For I rejoiced greatly when brethren came and testified of the truth that is in you, just as you walk in the truth. I have no greater joy than to hear that my children walk in truth." **Vs. 2 – 4**

What a parent, a teacher or good leader desires most is that they're children, their students and followers become prosperous and successful in what they have been taught. John takes great joy and comfort in what he has heard from other believers who had been to the church and their report. John had spent much of his life laboring with them that they might be able to live a life that is reflective of The Truth that Jesus had taught him.

"Beloved, you do faithfully whatever you do for the brethren, and for strangers, who have borne witness of your love before the church. If you send them forward on their journey in a manner worthy of God, you will do well. Because they went forth for His name's sake, taking nothing form the Gentiles. We therefore ought to receive such that we may become fellow worker for the truth." **Vs. 5 – 8**

The church has always taken care of those who minister and proclaim the Good News to others. That is the responsibility of the church and for the church fulfilling that responsibility; the church will be rewarded by God for doing what He has asked of them. Not only has this body of believers taken care of the ministers and missionaries that they knew but to those whom they did not know as well. They showed no favoritism. By doing so, the church became fellow labors in the work that these ministers and missionaries.

"I wrote to the church, but Diotrephes, who loves to have the preeminence among them does not receive us. Therefore, If I come, I will call to mind his deeds with he does, prating against us with malicious words. And not content with that, he himself does not receive the brethren, and forbids those who wish to putting them out of the church. Beloved, do not imitate what is evil, but what is good. He who does good is of God, but he who does evil has not seen God." **Vs. 9 – 11**

Diotrephes had position but he wanted preeminence. He felt as though he deserved praise and recognition for what he had done. The praise that he had received in the past apparently was not enough. John had been made aware of this and had written him about his error but Diothephes would have not of it and did not even acknowledge the rebuke in any way.

John tells Gaius, that if he comes he will address Diothrphes to his face and remind him of his evil words and deeds that he had unleashed. This power struggle of Diothrphes was not solely with John but with any other person in the church who might disagree with him. He had even excommunicated some members from this fellowship of believer.

To the remaining believers of this church John tells Gaius that they must resist evil intentions and not be inclined to pattern themselves after those who practice evil things. The pattern must be a good and kind pattern. John had written in his first epistle that if anyone did not love his brother, then it was proof that he did not know God in the first place. *"He who does not love does not know God, for God is love."* **1 John 4:8 NKJV** *"If someone says, 'I love God" and hates his brother, he is a liar; for he who does not love his brother whom he has seen, how an he love God whom he has not seen."* **1 John 4:20 NKJV**

"Demetrius, has a good testimony from all, and from the truth itself. And we also bear witness, and you know that our testimony is true." **Vs. 12**

John give a good example to follow and that is Demeterius. Demeterius had proven himself as faithful and true to the call of Christ. Demeterius was known by the church there and was known to John and others and everyone held Demeterius in high regard.

The believer today must test others before they follow them. The believer must question them and after a careful examination then they can be followed. We must hold true to The Truth and we must be led by the Holy Spirit's direction in our life in this world.

"I had many things to write, but I do not wish to writ to you with pen and ink; but I hope to speak face to face. Peace to you. Our friends greet you. Greet the friends by name." **Vs. 13 & 14**

John closes with the expression of his intentions to come to them soon. He had many things to share with them but those things would take time. We also ought to desire to be with fellow believers of the past and share with them the many things that have concerned us. We should care for them, we ought to pray for them and we should have a loving desire to fellowship with them in love.

We have mutual friend and with those mutual friends we ought to single them out by name and by the personal needs that each may have. We ought to desire the peace of God for each of them. We ought to love them. If we do we can keep each other true to The Truth.

Just the Basics

Discovering the Truth in an Untruthful World

Jude

By
Danny Glenn Thomas

Introduction

"The task of the scholar is to guarantee the purity of the text; to get as close as possible to the word as originally given. He may compare Scripture with Scripture until he discovers the true meaning of the text, but right there his authority ends. He must never sit in judgment upon what is written. He must not bring the meaning of the word before the bar of his reason." **A. W. Tozar**

Jude, also called Judas, is the brother of James and they were the half-brothers of Jesus. **Matthew 13:54 – 56 NKJV** *"When He had come to His own country, He taught them in their synagogue, so that they were astonished and said, 'Where did this man get the wisdom and these mighty works? Is this not the carpenter's son? Is not His mother called Mary? And His brothers James, Joses [or Joseph] Simon, and Judas? And His sisters, are they not all with us? where then did the Man get all these things?").*

Jude's humility is displayed by his reference to himself and also his sincere dedication to the ministry of the Good News of God by his acknowledgment of position in Christ Jesus. Neither James nor Jude make claims to Jesus as their brother but their Lord and Savior.

Jude wrote his Epistle or letter to follow up on the warnings of Peter because the Gnostics were now already infiltrating the early church and causing great turmoil and confusion to the body of Christ. Much of the text is identical to the words that Peter used and therefore Jude continues by warning these members of a local church of a coming attack by stealth and therefore exhorting them to be strong and "contend" or standup for the faith.

Jude's letter is short but powerful in warning and in his challenge to the believers then and even more so today.   Jude is short and is not given any chapter numbers only 25 verses.

The Letter

"Jude, a bondservant of Jesus Christ, and brother of James," **Vs 1**

Though he and Jesus had the same mother, Jude does not use that relationship to be the foundation of his authority, his authenticity is in his personal choice to be a bondservant or bond-slave of Jesus Christ.

A "bondservant" and "bond-slave" is a person who had been a slave to his master and been pleasing to his master and for his faithfulness his master has given him his freedom. But rather than to take advantage of this freedom the once slave now freed desires to stay with his master because of the love and admiration that he has for him. **Exodus 21:5 & 6** *"But if the servant plainly says, 'I love my master, my wife, and my children, I will not go out free.' Then his master shall bring him to the judges. He shall also bring him to the door or to the doorpost, and his master shall pierce his ear, with an awl, and he shall serve him forever."* **NKJV**

Jude considered himself a "bondservant" of Jesus. His desire, his purpose in life is to do the bidding of His "Savior" Jesus Christ. This is to be our desire as believers as well; our freedom is in Christ Jesus; our reason for living is for the desire of Christ Jesus and He is our Lord.

Jude was also the brother of James, the writer of the Book of James and Apostle of Jesus Christ. James, in like manor of his brother Jude or Judas (not Judas Iscariot the son of Simon Iscariot **John 13:26**); James refers himself as a "bondservant" **James 1:1**

Jude does call himself as the Jude who is the brother of James. This is the writer of this Epistle or letter.

"To those who are called, sanctified by God the Father, and preserved in Jesus Christ." **Vs. 2**

The recipients of this letter are those who are sanctified by God or those who are followers of the Son of God, Jesus. They have been set apart from others of the world as a recipient of God's displayed love. This is a great blessing and the reason for the blessing is because they have believed in God's Son; they have repented of their sins; they have been cleansed of those sins because of the righteousness of Jesus. **2 Corinthians 5:21** *"For He made Him who knew no sin to be sin for us, that we might become the righteousness of God in Him."* **NKJV**

Not only has the believer been sanctified, set apart or "reserved" as a recipient of God's great love but he has also been *"preserved"*. To preserve something, requires something to be added, something beyond the natural ability to last. Jesus has preserved us "eternally". On our own we will die in our sin but because of the cleansing preservative of the blood of Jesus Christ and His righteousness, the believer is sanctified and preserved eternally. Because of the righteous blood of Jesus Christ applied to the believer, eternal death is replaced with eternal life. No longer does the sting of eternal death have its hold on the believer. The believer is reserved for eternal life in heaven with Jesus. Yes the believer is reserved and preserved by the acts of God.

"Mercy, peace and love be multiplied to you." **Vs. 2**

Mercy can only be given by someone superior to the other. Mercy is defined as "not giving" someone what they deserve. What mankind deserves is judgment based upon his sin or falling short of God's requirement of perfection. God requires and demands all His creation to be perfect, He requires purity and holiness. None of those requirements and demands can be met by mankind therefore, something must be added to mankind in order to justify God from unleashing His righteous and just punishment.

The answer is mercy and mercy is justly given for a person accepting the sacrifice or His Only Begotten Son at Calvary; for believing that Jesus was God's Son and that God raised Him from the grave. Because of mankind's faith and trust God acts in mercy the immediate reaction of the believer is God's peace. There is no longer any reason for fear, because we are now "in Christ Jesus" and in Christ Jesus there is no fear. That peace that is felt is because of the love that defines Jesus. *"Jesus answered and said to him, 'If anyone love Me, he will keep My word; and My Father will love him, and We will come to him and make Our home with him."* **John 14:23 NKJV**

This mercy, peace and love is God's mercy, peace, and love; it is applied to the believer because God desires to do it and goes all through the believer. This mercy, peace and love of God intensifies and grows, or it "multiplies" and they explode within the believer and cannot be explained but graciously experienced by the believer and it isn't a conditional mercy but a gracious application of mercy.

"Beloved, while I was very diligent to write to you concerning our common salvation, I found it necessary to write to you exhorting you to contend earnestly for the faith with which was once for all delivered to the saints." **Vs. 3**

Jude had been desiring to write to these believers out of his joy he had because of the common and genuine salvation that they shared. Jude writes this letter out of his greater concern regarding the situation that was in the church. This problem was not exclusive to the church there but that same difficulty was also common in other bodies of believers. This was a great danger that they needed to be aware and there were specific steps that needed to be put into action for the sake of the cause of Christ.

"For certain men have crept in unnoticed, who long ago were marked out for this condemnation, ungodly men, who turn the grace of our God into lewdness and deny the only Lord God and our Lord Jesus Christ." **Vs. 4**

What was at stake was that common salvation that came through Jesus Christ. There were specific or certain teachers and preachers who have made it their aim to destroy that common salvation. These people who were now in the church were those whom Peter had written about, who would be coming into the church. **2 Peter 2:1 - 2**. Peter had warned that they would be coming and Jude warns that they are now among them; they are there.

They have "crept" in, they made their entrance and at first were hardly noticed but as time went on they became more and more prominent, known and even trusted. These people are the ungodly men and women of Satan himself. They are the "thieves" that Jesus spoke of whose desire is to kill, steal and destroy. **John 10:10**

The come thinking that they might conquer but they have already lost because God has already secured their judgment, their punishment in a prepared place for them along with Satan and his angels. **Matthew 25:4; Revelation 20:12 – 15; 2 Peter 2:4 - 11**

Jude tells us of their purpose and desire is to turn the grace of God into a lewd, disgraceful practice. They promote the idea that if you have been forgiven for your sin and God's grace is upon you, then you can do anything you desire to do. You can do anything because you have been forgiven and you should enjoy yourself on this earth, doing anything you desire.

This unholy teaching is despicable and unworthy of Holy God. They even deny that God is Who He says He is. The specific teaching then was the Gnostic Gospel which emphases and proclaims a special knowledge which is the main thing to have and if you have this knowledge you are separated from the rest of the world and can do as you wish. They deny that The Father, The Son and The Holy Spirit are one, they do not believe that Jesus is God.

Be careful today dear believer for God is not mocked, He is not to be dishonored but He is to be worshipped in spirit and truth. He alone is holy and worthy to be praised. Don't listen to anyone who might tell you otherwise. Test the spirits!

"But I want to remind you, though you once knew this, that the Lord, having saved the people out of the land of Egypt, afterward destroyed those who did not believe."

It was only Joshua, Caleb and those under the age of 20 who came out of Egypt that actually entered into the promised-land. The others were denied because of unbelief; every one of them died in the wilderness and did not enter the promised-land.

The reminder is for all believers. Peter had warned of approaching danger in **2 Peter 2:1 – 3** and now Jude warns that they have now arrived in the church. With his warning of the false teachers he also informs the believers that these infiltrators are known by God and He has already set their judgment. God knew them before the foundations of the world and has already determined and set their judgment.

Jude is saying that we ought to learn from history and benefit from that knowledge. The believer must remember that God is always in control regardless of what the situation may happen to be and don't allow our situation to cause us to doubt and lose faith in God and therefore lose our joy in life and be in danger of losing eternal rewards or be destroyed because of unbelief. The Children of Israel in their exodus from Egypt are the example, they died not receiving their reward.

"And angels who did not keep their proper domain, but left their own abode, He has reserved in everlasting chains under darkness for the judgment of the great day;"
Vs. 6

Another example of God's judgment is Satan and the angels whom he carried with him in his revolt, we know the number of revolting angels were one third of all the angels in heaven: **(Revelation 12:4, 7 - 9** *"His tail drew a third of the stars of heaven and threw them to the earth. And the dragon stood before the woman who was ready to give birth, to devour her Child was caught up to God... And war broke out in heaven: Michael and his angels fought with the dragon; and the dragon and his angels fought, but they did not prevail, nor was a place found for them in heaven any longer. So the great dragon was cast out, that serpent of old, called the Devil and Satan, who deceives the whole world, he was cast to the earth, and his angels were cast out with him."* **NKJV; Matthew 25:41** *"then He will also say to those on the left hand, 'Depart from Me, you cursed, into the everlasting fire prepared for the devil and his angels;"* **NKJV**)

These detestable people, these false prophets, are already judged and awaiting their day of judgment, the sentence will be carried out at the appointed time and last for eternity. The believer must keep this in mind and not lose heart but trust and watch. How does one watch? A believer doesn't blindly accept any teaching but he lays that teaching alongside Scripture and compares it, testing the spirits whether they are genuinely of God. Trust is earned not deserved and never trust that which will affect eternity. **1 John 4:1** *"Beloved, do not believe every spirit, but test the spirits, whether they are of God; because many false prophets have gone out into the world."* **NKJV**

"as Sodom and Gomorrah, and the cities around them in a similar manner to these, having given themselves over to sexual immorality and gone after strange flesh, are set

forth as an example, suffering vengeance of eternal fire." **Vs. 7**

The cities of Sodom and Gomorrah are stark reminders and examples of the impending judgment of God upon sin. I'm sure the citizens of the cities felt secure, nor had little if any fear of God, but judgment came, it came quickly and the judgment was total. Sodom and Gomorrah were not alone in the judgement but the cities and communities around them were guilty of the same great sins and they suffered the judgment of God as well. Sin will infest all who are around.

Peter makes mention that "righteous Lot" had his righteous soul "tormented" by the daily grievous sin of all around him. **2 Peter 2:8** The believer must take heed of the sin around us and all teaching around them that does agree 100% with Scripture. The believer must expose false teaching and choose to leave it.

"Likewise, also these dreamer defile the flesh, reject authority, and speak evil of dignitaries." **VS. 8**

One glowing characteristic of false teachers is they are great dreamers or talk about dreams from God to them about things that they have been chosen to do or to have a new revelation from God. Yet with this new revelation from God they seem to have no problem to live a life style that is totally against all the Scripture promotes. They have no respect for authority or leaders of any type. They seem to be the sole leader.

"Yet, Michael the archangel, in contending with the devil, when he disputed about the body of Moses, dared not

bring against him a reveling accusation, but said, The Lord rebuke you!" **Vs. 9**

Jude, a Jew and well familiar with Jewish books of Scripture refers to the apocryphal book *"The Assumption of Moses"* where the story of Michael the arch angel sought to bury the body of Moses but the Devil disputed with him saying that Moses was a murder and therefore, that he, Satan, had authority over Moses' body. Rather than condemn Satan for his slander, Michael claimed the Lord God to be discipliner and judge.

The believer is no match for demons, much less Satan himself. The believer should never at any time wish or speak words of judgment against anyone because he goes beyond his own authority in doing so. The believer doesn't judge, the believer obeys and follows God.

"But these speak evil of whatever they do not know; and whatever they know naturally, like brute beasts, in these things they corrupt themselves." **Vs. 10**

These false teachers are evil and they only know how to speak evil against others, they are like animals that merely respond in a natural instinctive. These false teachers react to a stimulus with a natural response and with little or no thought. Their instinctive manner is one of the flesh not the manner of the Spirit of Truth. Though they may know Scripture, Satan tempts them or tests them with twisted or improperly used Scripture as he did with Jesus in the wilderness. **Matthew 4:1 –11**

We must remember that just because someone uses Scripture, that in itself does not give them credibility. Scripture must be used properly; God gives credibility through His Holy Spirit and His Word confirms it. God's Spirit bears witness with our spirit and our spirit must bear witness with others confirming them to be of like spirit. **Romans 8:16** *"The Spirit Himself bears witness with our spirit that we are children of God,"* **NKJV 1 Corinthians 2:10** *"But God has revealed them to us through His Spirit. For the Spirit searches all things, yes, the deep things of God."* **NKJV** 1 **Thessalonians 5:21** *"Test all things; hold fast what is good."* **NKJV**

"Woe, to them! For they have gone in the way of Cain, have run greedily in the error of Balaam for profit, and perished in the rebellion of Korah." **Vs. 11**

The example of life for these people to follow is that of Cain, which is a covetous spirit and a selfish, and enviousness of others. They set greed as their goal in life like that of the false prophet Balaam and they seek only personal prophet for themselves at the expense of others. They are rebellious to the direct commands and will of God and their infectious evil desires spreads to others. Beware of them and take note from their reward, which is the anger and wrath of a just God.

"These are spots in your love feasts, while they feast with you without fear, serving only themselves. They are clouds without water, carried about by the winds; late autumn trees without fruit, twice dead, pulled up by the roots; raging waves of the sea, foaming up their own shame; wandering stars for whom is reserved the blackness of darkness forever." **Vs. 12 & 13**

These false prophets and teachers do not deliver what they claim or what you expect them to deliver, which is truth. They join you in your celebration of Jesus Christ and participate in worship and seem to have the same joy as you do and you may even be impressed by the display of sincerity but they are empty. Like a spot on a clean cloth they are very noticeable but they are there for their own benefit not to benefit others. They examples that Jude give are four fold:

1. The example of clouds: You need rain and they seem to be carrying rain but they blow over and leave nothing.

2. The example of late blooming fruit trees: You keep looking for fruit but they have none. They are dead as far as their fruit is concerned and they will be pulled up because of the barrenness, twice dead.

3. The example of the churning wave: The wave looks clean but as it breaks upon the beach it churns up all the refuse, dirt and sand of the beach.

4. The example of the wandering star: Stars produce light and are constantly holding their position and dependable for navigation but there are shooting stars and comets burning out and falling out of their constellation into the blackness of the vast universe. Jude could also be referring to the angels who fell from heaven with the fall of Satan.

"Now Enoch, the seventh from Adam, prophesied about these men also, saying 'Behold, the Lord comes with ten thousand of His saints, to execute judgment on all, to

convict all who are ungodly among them of all their ungodly deeds which they have committed in an ungodly way, and of all the harsh things which ungodly sinners have spoken against Him.'" **Vs. 14 & 15**

Enoch walked with God and was taken by God, we read in **Genesis 5:24.** Enoch was the son was Methuselah who lived to be 969 years of age. On the day that Methuselah died the flood came upon the earth. Sin had ravaged the earth so that the only followers of God at that time were merely eight people, Noah and his family.

Jude refers to the Enoch here as proclaiming the judgment of God upon the earth. In the apocryphal book of **1 Enoch 1:9** we read this account. The Lord comes with ten thousands of his set apart one to execute judgment. As the whole earth was judged with water it will be judged with unquenchable fire. As in the days of Noah and Enoch so it will be when the Jesus returns. People do not get away with their sins and rebellious deeds; in the end God wins. Remember that!

"These are grumblers, complainers, walking according to their own lusts; and they mouth great swelling words, flattering people to gain advantage." **Vs. 16**

These false prophets and teachers are never satisfied with any one or anything that may go against them and their personal goal. They grumble and complain about everything. They are cunning, gifted in speech and dangerous. They know how to use others to bring about their desired goal.

"But you, beloved, remember the words which were spoken before by the apostles of our Lord Jesus Christ: how

they told you that there would be mockers in the last time who would walk according to their own ungodly lust." **Vs. 18**

Jude wants to jog their memory about other writings from other apostles such as Paul, Peter and James who had also given them warning about these cunning people. The desire of these false prophets and teachers are in opposition to the fruits of the Spirit. **Galatians 5:16 – 26**

They must remember:
- What they have been taught
- What they have been warned against and what to expect.
- Remember that they are "not" like you and do not have your desires.

"These are sensual persons, who cause divisions, not having the Spirit." **Vs. 19**

The Spirit of the Lord brings liberty, unity, peace and love for one another. **2 Corinthians 3:17**

Liberty, unity, peace and love do not divide they bring together for the benefit of all. If any of these are absent from a teacher or preacher, then they are not preachers and teachers of the Truth.

"But you, beloved, building yourselves up on your most holy faith, praying in the Holy Spirit, keep yourselves in the love of God, looking for the mercy of our Lord Jesus Christ unto eternal life." **Vs. 20 & 21**

You, the true believer must continue to build up and strengthen your lives in the truth. The believer must never consider prayer as not important. We all need to pray, at all times and about everything. **Philippians 4:6** *"Be anxious for nothing, but in everything by prayer and supplication, with thanksgiving, let your requests be made known to God."* Letting your requests be made known to God does not mean, informing God of them but giving God the position He deserves in your life. It's like talking with your dad about a problem you have and you know that he knows about it already. That brings comfort.

Staying close to God, is drawing near God and Satan will flee. **James 4:3** Jude encourages the believer to be clothed in the love of God because love covers a multitude of sins and love conquers. **James 5:20** *"let him know that he who turns a sinner from the error of his way will save a soul from death and cover a multitude of sins."* **NKJV**; **1 Peter 4:8** *"and above all things have fervent love for one another, for love will cover a multitude of sins."* **NKJV**

Mercy is not giving to another something that they deserve. Mercy is not given by the weak but the strong. Mercy and grace is given to the believer or to whom ever He desires to give it. God and in His mercy and grace has given the believer eternal life. We ought to show mercy, grace and love to others. We, in turn ought to proclaim the Good News to others of God's great gift.

"And on some have compassion, making a distinction, but others save with fear, pulling them out of the fire, hating even the garment defiled by the flesh." **Vs. 22 & 23**

There are some whom we need to have more compassion than others, those who desperately need our help. Some believers who fall to various sins need our aggressive pursuit for them in order to rescue and recover them from the impending danger and fire that is quickly coming upon them and will soon engulf them.

We ought to show mercy to the non-believer as we share the Good News but we must also be cautious not to be caught up in their sins. We read in **2 Peter 2:7 & 8** *"and delivered righteous Lot, who was oppressed by the filthy conduct of the wicked (for that righteous man, dwelling among them, tormented his righteous soul from day to day by seeing and hearing their lawless deeds).* **NKJV**

"Now to Him who is able to keep you from stumbling, And to present you faultless before the presence of His glory with exceeding joy, to God our Savior Who alone is wise, be glory and majesty, Dominion and power, both now and forever. Amen." **Vs. 24 & 25**

With this marvelous and great Doxology Jude closes his epistle or letter. Give God glory in all things and give Him glory at all times. Thank Him for all things and in all things. Even in difficulties we will find the all present God, reach out for Him and take His extended hand and glory that He is there.

Give God control of your life by submitting to Him in every area of your life and at all the times in your life, He wants to guide us and to lead us. God is the only one who can keep us from falling, so stay near Him. Draw near to God and He will draw near to you **James 4:7 & 8**.

Give God glory because He alone deserves glory. **Revelation 4:11** *"you are worthy, O Lord, to receive glory and honor and power, For You created all things, and by Your will they exist and were created."* **NKJV** God alone is God and beside Him there is no other. **Deuteronomy 4:35; Psalm 86:10**

God alone provided our salvation through His only begotten Son Jesus Christ and there is no other Salvation. **Acts 4:12** This salvation is God's idea, it is His plan and we have nothing to do with His offer of salvation to us. **2 Corinthians 5:17 – 21** *"Therefore, if anyone is in Christ, he is a new creation; old things have passed away; behold, all things have become new. Now all things are of God, who has reconciled us to Himself through Jesus Christ, and has given us the ministry of reconciliation, that is that God was in Christ reconciling the world to Himself, not imputing their trespasses to them, and has committed to us the word of reconciliation. Now then, we are ambassadors for Christ, as though God were pleading through us: we implore you on Christ's behalf, be reconciled to God. For He made Him who knew no sin to be sin for us, that we might become the righteousness of God in Him."* **NKJV**

- Glory is His alone.
- Majesty is His alone.
- Power is His alone.
- Authority comes from Him alone.
- It's always been this way
- That is the way it is now
- That is the way it will always be.
- As it is written, so shall it be!

www.ingramcontent.com/pod-product-compliance
Lightning Source LLC
Chambersburg PA
CBHW060154070426
42447CB00033B/1327